BRIEN MASTERS is qualified both as a State and Waldorf teacher, and has taught everything from Choir to Chemistry to Creative Writing. He teaches around the world and has acted as a consultant up to government ministerial level. He has written numerous articles and several publications for use in schools, and his Doctoral thesis is a critical appraisal of Waldorf praxis in the light of Rudolf Steiner's original educational ideas. Brien Masters is presently Director of the London Waldorf Teacher Training Seminar, as well as a new seminar in Gran Canaria.

GW00374510

BY THE SAME AUTHOR

STEINER EDUCATION AND SOCIAL ISSUES

How Waldorf schooling addresses the problems of society

Brien Masters

Sophia Books

Sophia Books
Hillside House, The Square
Forest Row, East Sussex
RH18 5ES

Published by Sophia Books 2007
An imprint of Rudolf Steiner Press

A catalogue record for this book is available from the British Library

ISBN 978 1 85584 200 7

Cover by Andrew Morgan Design
Typeset by DP Photosetting, Neath, West Glamorgan
Printed and bound in Great Britain by Cromwell Press Limited,
Trowbridge, Wiltshire

Contents

CHILDREN AND TEACHERS

TEACHER-PUPIL, TEACHER-COLLEAGUE, TEACHER-PARENT RELATIONSHIPS

Introduction

One of the most recent tsunamis to strike the educational shores of the UK and USA was the Unicef-instigated 'Report Card 7, Child Poverty in Perspective: An Overview of Child Well-being in Rich Countries'. Ironically, the report was made public on Valentine's Day (2007), since those who need the most love for their well-being—the children in our midst—are revealed as getting an overwhelmingly poor deal. The UK ranks easily as the worst place to raise children, coming lowest out of 21 countries under the headings: poverty and inequality, health and safety, education, family and friendships, sex, drink and drugs, happiness. This is despite the country being one of the 'strongest' economies in the world. There was no doubt in the comments of numerous experts about the report's robustness; its author, Professor Jonathan Bradshaw, Professor of Social Policy, University of York, has an international reputation for his work and is a leading expert in his field.

While the report is, perhaps, the severest indictment to date of the UK's track record on child care in its broadest sense, it would, of course, be unfair to lumber education solely with the blame. Clearly, education per se can do little to alleviate poverty directly or to turn the tide of the kind of family life that is unsupportive of childhood. However, family and other human disasters stem from attitudes that obviously cannot be attributed to the newborn baby. Nor do they spring up from nowhere, unbidden, in the adult. Between birth and adulthood is childhood. The present generation of adults surely owes the attitudes that seem to be drastically failing children in some measure, large or small, to their own educational upbringing. Ditto with the previous generation and so on—back up the slippery slope!

Yet when the news of the report first broke, only one out of all the experts who were asked to comment by *The Independent*, Dr Richard House, a lecturer in psychotherapy and counselling at the University of Roehampton, thought that 'the education system adds to children's unhappiness, in terms of testing. Children's love of learning gets compromised.' Other remarks, however, had serious implications for the educator. The Dutch, who ranked highest in the report, strongly advocated a child-friendly society that started in the early years and extended throughout childhood, avoiding any 'pressure' to achieve until children enter their teens. Dr Gerrit Breusma, head of development psychology at the University of Groningen pointed to the centuries-old tradition of child-centred families in Holland as evidenced in the genre paintings of seventeenth-century Dutchman Jan Steen. This contrasts strongly with a society that hankers after affluence at all costs, in which political success depends on it, and in which childhood is little more than a conduit for sifting out those 'brains' that will produce the goods.

We know from the Child Exploitation and Online Protection Centre, and from other sources, of the trafficking of children from countries like China, Vietnam, Afghanistan, Nigeria and Eritrea, for absorption in prostitution rings, street crime, drug smuggling, use in cannabis production factories and domestic slavery—and we are outraged. Yet our awareness and consciousness appear numb when it comes to what seems tantamount to the enslavement of childhood in much of western education systems and lifestyles.

It seems evident that in the West (or rather, the west of the West, though not Canada) the deterioration in certain social values—running parallel with the advance in technological achievement and the acquisition of wealth—has a long history. It is not, of course, a matter now of reversing the situation. We are where we are. Nevertheless, it is my contention in the present work that (a) it is *education* that has a central role to play (perhaps *the* central role) in bringing into human lives those qualities that can take us forward into a progressive future; and that (b) Rudolf Steiner's educational approach, as being put into practice mainly in the Waldorf schools across the world, is well equipped to do this.

Clearly it is asking a lot of education to inaugurate changes in attitudes of this order. That is:

- to *help reclaim childhood* where it has been corrupted, abandoned or even quashed through ill-advised practices and methods of education;
- to *engender self-confidence* in children by avoiding the inevitable 90-plus per cent rate of failure to achieve the top grades, in an educational culture driven by competitive assessment;
- to *uncover and further instil an inner stability* in children where homes are broken, nations are at war, streets are unsafe and terrorism is both a concrete threat and a constant drum-roll in the media;
- to *reinstate the human* in a world whose cyberspace-tinted spectacles are in danger of limiting all vision, and where the chemical industry jealously guards a large measure of dominion over birth, death, nutrition, agriculture, health, climate and other aspects of life;
- to *rediscover and restore balance* in life where cognitional intelligence increasingly dismisses emotional, moral and other forms of intelligence;

- to *reawaken a sensitivity for and valuing of the qualitative* where factual knowledge has largely monopolized people's minds;
- to *combat the hydra-headed negative effects of materialism*, such as substance abuse, the adultification of childhood, uninspiring, test-driven school lessons, video games and junk food with its ever more ubiquitous counterpart in the couch potato;
- to *put supportive alternatives in the place* where, through society's changing consciousness, 'boundaries' in children's lives have disappeared;
- to *present inspiring role models* alongside the absence of such on children's own doorsteps, and in place of the promiscuity and eccentricities of many prominent celebrities and media 'stars';
- to *motivate a genuine will to work*, in place of the cat-o'-nine-tails of competitive culture with which we flog our youngsters at all levels;
- to *cultivate a sense of discrimination and proportion* that will withstand the hype and peer pressure that surrounds dress and other personal possessions;
- to *implant a feeling of self-fulfilment*, and the inner stability it engenders, which would otherwise be swept away by the tornado of electronic entertainment that has left soul destruction and destitution in its wake and annihilated simple, creative enjoyment of the natural world;
- to *help heal the wound* caused by fatherlessness, in single-parent families, often deemed to be the cause of behavioural problems;
- to *sow the seeds of, and encourage the search for, rounded human wisdom* to counteract the vacuum of internet surfing;
- to *build up a dignified and progressive picture of the human being* as an antidote to the prevalence of absurdly infantilized

adults, and the over-sexed images of all kinds flouted on screen, spread across children's literature, and manifest in much toy design;

- to *pre-empt* those forces which lead to child depression, child suicide, and the fear of paedophiles that is drummed into children's consciousness, which sets up inhibiting and potentially damaging barriers between them and X, Y and Z whom they will encounter at the bus stop, the supermarket checkout and other public places;
- to *reverse* the disappearance of imagination in real play;
- to *rekindle* feelings of self-esteem, care for material things and consideration for others, in place of the growing lack of respect for self, the environment and fellow human beings;
- to *bring order* into the social chaos that lurks at every street corner;
- to *cultivate anew* the field of emotional intelligence which, in our modern climate, has become fallow and often neglected;
- to *endow the soul with new sources of moral strength* where crime is on the rampage and the bankruptcy of religious life in so many of its forms has taken its toll.

An impossible task? (And the list does not claim to be comprehensive.) Obviously it is overwhelmingly impossible to achieve in one lightning step, certainly if education were single-handed—the home and society as a whole must play their part. But human childhood is a lengthy affair and offers the educationist incomparable scope to discover, investigate and understand *the whole child* and thence work towards a well-tuned, well-directed, scientifically and artistically developed pedagogy. Such pedagogy cannot be delivered by computer software, activated by a surveillance culture or by the contrivers of party-political programmes. It depends on the human being in the classroom who is professionally trained in truly child-centred pedagogy and who is continually developing her own creative capacities that will enable her to rise to each new occasion that crops up, rears its ugly head, challenges her courage, defies her ideals, and perhaps even threatens burnout. No one is pretending that education is a sinecure.

In the early days of the first Waldorf School in Stuttgart, it was not only Steiner himself who spoke publicly about education: the teachers in the school would also be requested to give talks about their work and the approach the school was taking towards education. When his advice was sought about what lines to take, Steiner was short and to the point: Tell them what's wrong and what Waldorf is doing about it. (Or words to that effect.)

To my knowledge, the archives have not yielded any stenographic reports that would indicate if and how the teachers followed his advice. To do so today would not be an easy tightrope to walk. Be too harsh about identifying 'What's wrong' and there would be the danger of appearing too ungrateful, of assigning blame, of assuming the high moral ground, of over-indulging in value judgements. Give the impression that Waldorf has the unassailable answer, and there will be the danger that its back will constantly be beaten with its own rod, particularly if the view it takes and the aims it claims to achieve are presented arrogantly.

However, the current clamour of voices saying what is failing childhood in the education system itself, along with those educational outcomes that manifest all too blatantly in society as a whole, obviates the necessity for Waldorf to do more than cite this or that report, or this or that incident symptomatic of the times in which we live. For example, it was Lord Richard Layland, Director of the Well-being Programme at the Centre for Economic Performance and London School of Economics, who, following the Unicef report, pointed to research suggesting that despite everything that has been put into schemes such as Personal Social and Health Education (PSHE), and similar, we are 'no happier' than we were 50 years ago. Notwithstanding the seriousness with which Lord Layland viewed this, it is incumbent on Waldorf—and this is directly linked with the second part of Steiner's advice (what Waldorf is doing to address the problems)—to offer a diagnosis which could lead to an educational solution. *Why* is Britain deemed to be the worst place in which to be a child out of the 21 most affluent countries in the world?

Research tends to locate and affirm amply *where* the problem lies. Children are bored at school, lonely, unhappy, pressurized, robbed of their childhood, dropping out of school at the earliest provocation and leaving home with low skills, lacking a sense of well-being, failed by their families, poor in human relationships, prone to addictions, unimaginative, unkind and unhelpful, fearful of getting mugged or being bullied, irritated by police presence, suffering from a sense of failure, becoming more and more obese, 'cruelly' subjected (i.e. prematurely) to the 3 Rs when they 'should be playing in the sunshine', made into the victims of our 'frenzy' for competition, and so on and so forth—and in all this I am doing absolutely no more than picking out some of the 'currants' from *one* newspaper on *one* day, albeit the black Wednesday when news of Unicef's report broke. But what are the deep-seated *causes*?

Social workers, of course, thankfully at all levels, will go on valiantly doing their jobs and no doubt with renewed efforts. And others will address the issues in one way or another. *But the horse has bolted.* Unless we realize that the stable door needs urgent attention, we are likely to be forced to continue chasing bolted horses and, when we've located their whereabouts, having to deal with their mouth-foaming wildness while we, meanwhile, are breathless from the chase and with barely an adequate bridle to hand.

Steiner's educational answer was, and always will be (a) to research and research and go on researching the true, complex and full nature of the human being in childhood, i.e. the first three *septennial* phases;★ and (b) to develop and harness—no extended metaphor intended!—perceptive, understanding, creative, caring and imaginative faculties in the human being as teacher, which are capable of addressing the evolving needs of the child. By teaching in a way that is prophylactic, that equips the child for the so-called real world in an appropriate way, we can enhance those qualities in all young individuals whereby, throughout life, they can direct their destinies with a lively sense of purpose and personal fulfilment.

It becomes immediately evident that this approach to education cannot be set out in check-list format. It is essentially an *art*. We don't walk around the art galleries or the auction rooms with a handbook checking, inspector-like, whether Rembrandt did this in that order, and that in this order. Nevertheless, the artist's materials *are* material. On the one hand, artists use their materials in an ever-explorative way; on the other hand, whatever their genius they still have

---

★ The septennial (or seven-year) phases of human development is a concept which Steiner elaborated at considerable length and seemingly inexhaustibly. It is fundamental to the understanding of his view of the *whole* child. The present text has recourse to it frequently, notably at pp. 15, 28, 31, 66, 99, 142f, 201.

to engage in the properties, characteristics and limitations of those materials.

Thus, in the first chapter of this book I set out in my own words what is the essential *nature of the child* as gradually revealed and described by Steiner's unprecedently advanced insight—though I naturally recoil from referring to the child as the educator's 'material', despite the above simile. In the subsequent chapters, more from *the teacher's perspective*, I relate and discuss personal experiences, that have bearing on the art of education as elaborated by Steiner and since put into practice by the vast spectrum of Waldorf schools and kindergartens across the world. In passing I also suggest how Waldorf principles and praxis might offer a remedy for many of society's underlying problems, and not just UK society at the bottom of the Unicef pile. If the globe is going to become a better place in which to live, *all so-called richer and poorer countries will need to create new cultural wealth,* and education must surely play a central role in this. But the question is (hands up!): *Which* education?

1. Steiner: A Revolutionary in Education

'His Feast Day is on November 13.'
I was at the last stage of preparing a London lecture entitled 'Education at the Abyss'. It was one of a series of lectures on the theme of what was *revolutionary* about Rudolf Steiner's ideas and the work that has arisen from them over the past 85 years and more. The lecture, scheduled earlier in the summer, came as it so happened just two months after a letter had been published in the *Daily Telegraph* (12 September 2006) about the sorry state of modern childhood. There were 110 signatories—including children's authors, professors of education, the Archbishop of Canterbury and others eminent in their field, of whom (wearing my Course Director of the London Waldorf Teacher Training Seminar hat) I was one.★

The letter, instigated by Dr Richard House, lecturer at Roehampton University, and Sue Palmer, author of *Toxic Childhood*, despite its battery of leading figures, had been turned down by *The Times* on the basis that it offered no solution to the malaise it was identifying. The solution could, of course, easily have been extrapolated from remarks taken from the words of the many signatories, but this was not enough for *The Times*. However, the second newspaper to be approached, the *Daily Telegraph*, seeing the import of the matter, rose above slick, one-day wonder journalism, produced an article on the theme (with the feisty headline 'Junk Culture is Poisoning our Children'), published the entire letter and included a leader in which the writer 'welcome[d] the debate on lost childhood prompted by this letter'. The

---

★ The text of the letter is reproduced in the Appendix, pp. 250f.

debate landslid across the media, including an interview on the *Today* programme at prime (breakfast) time and a considerable sharing of opinion on Radio 4's *Any Questions*. Within months, Richard House had responded to 18 requests for written articles in various papers and journals and had appeared on television to champion the cause.

Now one of the most perspicacious comments was: 'Today parents (often with the best of intentions) shower children with the *fruits of materialism* to such an extent that their minds are stunted, and the opportunity to enjoy the *simple outdoor life of play* that was once a child's perceived birthright is lost.' (The emphases are mine.) Such fruits certainly sound like the poisonous half of the apple that the wicked queen (stepmother) gave to Snow White, thus bypassing the security measures that the seven wise and well-meaning dwarfs had set up, as we learn from the familiar Grimms' *fairy tale*.

'Showered with the fruits' and 'lost childhood' sound contradictory at first hearing. It was surely in earlier ages, one might argue, that life encroached on childhood. Whether the family was poor (or peasant) and children had to put their shoulder to the plough or climb up the inside of chimneys or the family was educated and/or could afford it, childhood was guillotined at about 14 years of age—Shakespeare soon off to London attending the horses of the theatregoers, Mozart paraded round the courts of Europe as a protégé; Leonardo, Michelangelo, Benvenuto Cellini and dozens of other Renaissance artists apprenticed in the ateliers of their masters and so on. Until (to continue the argument) technological inventions started to 'save us time'—steam trains replacing slow horse-drawn vehicles, powered looms ousting slow (human speed) hand weaving, jumbo jets carting us through the air and cutting weeks off the circumnavigation of the globe on the high seas, the electric chair replacing the hangman's noose. And saving us personal energy: the electric toothbrush, bread kneading machines, the combine harvester, the deep freeze, the word counting facility in computer software, automatic doors, escalators, underfloor heating, the laser-beam 'conventional' weapons... Such liberated time and energy raising the so-called quality of life has surely enabled childhood to be extended. A high percentage of the population graduate in their early twenties without the faintest notion of what the inside of a chimney looks, smells or feels like—is soot in the hair better or worse than the coxcomb of a punk? And parents have time on their hands and money in the bank's hands to back up their credit cards, which enables them to lavish entertainment of one kind or another on the children's free evenings, weekends and long school holidays.

I have made the point and must stop being facetious. The tragedy that hijacked this potentially rosy and rewarding situation for parent and child deserves serious inspection. In Edmund Spenser's *The Faery Queen* (Book 1) it hardly needs the bard to tell us that the dragon's monstrous appearance 'bred cold, congealèd fear'. But Spenser still has reserves to bring out of the wings: the dragon's *breath* ('a cloud of smothering smoke and sulphur sear'). Psychologically this has the potential for intensifying the fear, but in fact its effect appears to spur the knight towards becoming the aggressor and, after considerable combat, the victor. It seems an odd analogy, but it is so close to the way the 'fruits of materialism' extended and *in the same breath*, so to speak, annulled childhood—'which to increase and all at once to kill', as the poet puts it—that it gives us insight into the seeming contradiction.

It is not necessary to go as far as labelling the fruits of

materialism as the 'work of the devil' (or whatever terminology we care to adopt). The chalice of concern, however,
has been overflowing for long enough. Here and there are
constructive legislative measures in response to the concern.
Here and there people are making valuable and successful
efforts—the creation of 'respect zones' in Newcastle-on-
Tyne is one of the latest. But predictably, none of it is enough
to stem the tide. A few (far too few, it seems) look to education for the answer, but one wonders to what extent it can
succeed in making any positive mark so long as education *in
its essence* is not in the hands of enlightened educators.

Steiner was certainly of that school of thought. He is
reputed to have remarked, when visiting England, 'In the
Waldorf School [...] we don't have any programmes: only
children and teachers.' What was he implying?

This seems tantamount to saying that not merely a new
direction was necessary, but a *completely new starting point*.
Perhaps justification for this extreme statement can be found
in the fact that orthodox education theory, to this day,
continues to omit the *teacher* from its four main headings:

(i)   the aims of education;
(ii)   the nature of the child;
(iii) the curriculum;
(iv)   the pedagogical method.

Many would argue, of course, that by implication, pedagogy
means that a person (the teacher, the pedagogue) is applying
the method, constantly coming up with creative pedagogical
ideas, on the spur of the moment even. Whether this argument stands up to education effected solely or principally by
means of computer software I shall leave on one side—and
certainly Steiner had plenty of advice to give about pedagogy. Notwithstanding, his starting point was emphatically

teachers and children. And in support of this, one only has to consider how many people's fondest memories of school are of lessons they enjoyed *because of the teacher*. Indeed, one can think of cases where her pedagogy even left something to be desired, compared with her colleagues. This made no difference: it was *her* lessons we enjoyed (and probably the ones whose content we subsequently remembered) that counted.

Each individual teacher having capacities that enable her teaching to be imbued with spontaneous creativity seems worlds apart from the surveillance ethos of the State sector which Estelle Morris came to deplore. On her retirement as Education Secretary in the Blair administration (2004) she agonized (using strong language, which here I am omitting): '[They, at No.10] think of an idea and then buzz off and think of another [while] I am busy delivering the last set of proposals.' Even allowing for a taste of 'sour grapes' in the language in which someone losing a place in the Cabinet expressed herself, the substance still remains.

★   ★   ★

Further light on the value that Steiner accorded the starting point 'children and teachers' can be shed by a consideration of how he obviously viewed the curriculum. He was abundantly aware of education through his tutoring activities already as a teenager, something in which he proved himself highly successful first and foremost for his pupils but also, incidentally, as a necessary means of subsistence. One suspects, his awareness was heightened either through direct contact and/or through a process of osmosis with his professor of German literature, Karl Julius Schröer. The latter's essays on education are extant and have been made known through recent research. It would be going too far to say that they are a prototype for Steiner's amazingly comprehensive ideas on education—the sphere in which it could be said he had more input than any other, the school in Stuttgart alone growing quickly to some thousand pupils with a corresponding quota of teachers. Nevertheless, there was strong compatibility, Schröer being something of a slipway, so to speak, that led to the Waldorf autobahn. Even so, these two sources—his own practical experience and the influence of his senior at the outset of his career—appear of little significance beside the subsequent *research* he diligently carried out and profusely expounded in lectures, in meetings and in written form.

This body of his oeuvre falls essentially into three categories:

(i)   the first lectures (and connected booklet) on education in 1907;
(ii) the inductory lectures and workshops given to the teachers elect in preparation for the first Waldorf School in Stuttgart in August/September 1919;
(iii) a short remark made in Bern in the summer of 1924.

The output of 1919 is, of course, the Gulf Stream of Steiner education, which flowed on continuously for the remainder of Steiner's working life, both in Stuttgart and in other places in Germany as well as abroad. Its content can be taken essentially together with the first (1907) public lectures, the main emphasis by far being on the nature of the human being and how this unfolds in childhood. In keeping with Schröer's concept of 'lifelong learning', Steiner does not confine himself to the first three septennial phases, but straightway sees (a) life as a whole; and (b) life in our present age as part of an enormous alpha-to-omega, ongoing process in the evolution of human consciousness. It thus transpires that Steiner saw education not only as a vital contribution to the immediate present, but also as something to set against a minimum time scale of centuries. Those who point to the origin of Waldorf being about 90 years ago (with the implied reservation: 'Isn't it getting out of date by now?') should bear this in mind, especially the latter point. Which is not at all to give Waldorf *carte blanche* to dig itself into 1919 trenches.

Already in elaboration of Steiner's inductory courses, in the 70 teachers' meetings he attended between September 1919 and September 1924, as well as in other lecture courses longer or shorter, Steiner reveals that their original 'substance' is not something that needs replacing in order to keep pace with the times; instead it contains within itself ideas that can be dwelt on and further unfolded, thus leading in many cases to *increasing relevance* for modern times. This is not to rule out linguistically rephrasing some of the original expressions as occur in the so-called secondary literature.

★ ★ ★

The profoundest and most far-reaching example of the extended application of Steiner's ideas, perhaps, is the establishment and growth of the Waldorf Kindergarten movement across the world (at a recent count approximately 1500 strong), something that was hardly visible in Steiner's day. A further example is the remark made in the course of lectures given in Bern in the summer of 1924 regarding the three arts of speech, modelling and music. These, when practised assiduously, Steiner urged, enable the teacher to sharpen her own understanding of those entities in the human constitution less visible to ordinary sense perception. Without an appreciation of the deeper aspects of the child's nature, the schooling of them will at best be hit and miss, and at second best fall significantly short of the pupils' real needs, leaving them stunted in their development. And at worst it will be counter-productive, which may bring us close to connecting the ills of society with where they are undoubtedly rooted—and in some cases exclusively—*in education.*

Such subtleties are not, perhaps, what immediately strike the onlooker who first comes across Steiner's educational ideas and their praxis in Waldorf schools. For the newcomer it is the more obvious features that make the education distinctive: the utterly unreserved welcoming atmosphere of the Kindergarten 'space'; the two-hour main-lesson at the beginning of the day lasting all told for four weeks; the eight-year span of the so-called Lower School (ages 6/7–14+) in which the class is taught main-lesson (and some other lessons as a rule) by the same teacher; the quite strict chronological grouping of children in each class (which does not preclude the possibility of some streaming according to ability, say, in modern languages or some specialist concentration as with a senior orchestra); the absence of a head teacher and heads of department so that the responsibility for the well-being of the whole school is something that is felt to be shared by all (in addition, of course, to the personal responsibility for each individual's lessons, a matter of normal professional integrity); teacher-participation in the non-teaching facets of school life such as personally representing the public face of the school on open days and in correspondence, school finances, maintenance, parent relations, publicity, recruitment and appointments, interviewing potential pupils and so on (for all of which Steiner held that lessons benefited through being more effective).

There will be further distinctions, too, which may only be evident on closer inspection. Three diverse examples:

(i)   the uniquely modern nature of the curriculum (owing to the fact that it was only very broadly outlined it was possible to embrace the most vibrantly contemporary topics in some subjects, e.g. science, literature and current affairs, all within the overall principle of child-relatedness, of course);

(ii) the enormous wariness Steiner called upon regarding the introduction of literacy;

(iii) the obvious anguish that he experienced through the fact that the school's finances and facilities didn't stretch as far as was necessary to give adequate support to the young people's music education.

Some of these aspects of the education were revolutionary in their day—for example, the 'project' and even the concept of 'course work', which have since become prominent features of education, could be shown to be closely connected to Steiner's original ideas. Others have become revolutionary by remaining uncompromised in the face of various kinds of change—like the persistence of a gradual introduction to literacy, which has stood out like a Waldorf rock in the shifting sands of praxis in this respect in many countries. All the above, however, on their own would not add up to a foundation for education that would stand the test of time and cultural adaptation as has Waldorf. For this foundation it is necessary firstly to turn to how Steiner saw the *child*, the 'subject' to be educated, and secondly what he saw as the *teacher's potential* to play her central role in the child's whole development. To gain a reasonably comprehensive view of this, in this chapter I shall consider the four well-known components (members) of the human being to which Steiner returned time and again—the bodily nature, the life (or formative) forces, the soul nature, and the self—in the light of how education can assist all of them (the so-called *whole child*) in maturing towards adulthood in harmony with one another, and in such a way that the adult can pursue a healthy and spiritually robust process of lifelong learning. The rest of the book shifts the emphasis to the *nature of the teacher*—as the fifth component in education theory—and to her vocational responsibilities, albeit with intermittent reference back to the subject matter of this chapter, so as never to lose sight of the child.

The child's bodily nature vis-à-vis education

The common-or-garden 'strength and health' of the body is, in one sense, a prerequisite for other aspects of bodily development. Yet one only need think of the part nutrition plays in this to realize that it is an aspect the responsibility for which—school meals, where they are provided, notwith-standing—rests principally on the home. In addition to what was once a common-sense approach, Steiner expounds on plenty of uncommon insights scattered throughout his oeuvre and one can always point the enquiring parent in those directions. Whether it is the educationist's task to heighten parental awareness of the dangers of the kind of nutrition and lifestyle which lead to the increasingly worry-ing phenomenon of child obesity we shall bypass here in favour of aspects that are more directly affected by what happens in the classroom.

It may seem, in this respect, that Steiner drew attention to the obvious. In the first (seven) years of bodily growth the emphasis is on the development of the nerve-sense system, in the second period (7–14 years) the emphasis is on the respiratory/circulatory systems, and in the puberty/post-puberty period (14+) the bodily developmental emphasis is in the region of the metabolic, reproductive and limb systems. Styles of teaching and lesson activities that involve appropriate physical movement clearly support the third of these, a point to take particularly into account during those years where study requirements, especially for school-leaving qualifications, may entail a disproportionate amount of sitting at desks or in front of resource centre screens. This problem was at least recognized in earlier times through the ample provision of sports facilities, though whether the typical pre-war grammar school practice of one afternoon per week plodding and squelching through mud on the rugby field even began to address the issue *in real pedagogical terms* is open to question.

Nowadays, we hear a lot about schools selling their playing fields, and critics of these sales are clearly of the opinion that the loss of such sports facilities is yet another educational deprivation. Steiner's solution was to regard the activity of the *will* as a healthily proportionate, time-well-spent part of every day at school (crafts and gardening in particular), and in a more refined way a vital part of every lesson, however sedentary in its essential nature the mode of teaching the subject is at core. Here lies infinite scope for pedagogical creativity. The drastic step—which has attracted much educational comment—taken by the Thomas Deacon Academy in Peterborough recently seems a perverse variation on the theme. Although retaining its playing fields—the pupils have games twice a week—the Academy was reported as having cut out PE and all playground-type breaks to give more time for exam revision. Apart from half an hour for lunch, the pupils are therefore basically at their desks from 0845 to 1600 hrs three days a week. It is, of course, an extreme case, but the thinking behind it is arguably as common as weeds on a neglected allotment.

In the long term, however, possibly even more important than the above is the effect of education on the *nerve-senses*. Straightway at birth (even in the womb) the child's sensory organs are activated. A beneficial activation leads to fine sensibility. And there are the *two* opposite extremes: a deficiency of stimulation or a surfeit of sense impressions—not mutually exclusive. Many aspects of modern life, often taken for granted, are the subtle cause of *sense-malnutrition*: bland, tasteless, over-processed food (compared, say, with vegetables fresh from the garden); right-angle tyrannized, machine-made furniture (compared with the handmade cabinets, chairs and dressers that graced the homes of our forefathers); mass-produced utensils and domestic objects (compared with the artisan-crafted lampstands, brooches, stirring spoons or bedside rugs used by our ancestors); acres of walls and ceilings with 'perfect' mat finishes (compared, say, with the panelling or tapestries of old, or the lazuring of very recent times); and so forth. The other extreme is the bombardment of the senses: brutal decibel levels, nature-eliminating urbanization with its sky-effacing concrete blocks and forests of road signs and billboards, psychedelically coloured plastic toys and so on. The senses, battered from one side and starved of sense-richness from the other, thus resort to or indulge in compensatory feasting on sense-impoverished and sense-impoverishing objects and substances.

A school's potential for addressing this issue is to create an environment that is sense-rich in as many ways as possible (which shouldn't depend on affluence), particularly in the early years when the senses are developing at their most subtle level. This potential is not, of course, confined to the younger years but continues to a lesser degree until school leaving. In the middle years of schooling, it is a matter of teachers being the mediators between the world and the (by now) sensitively oriented sight, hearing, touch, etc. This occurs on the one hand through the teacher's verbal descriptions of the world: the accented *form* of animals (pig snout, giraffe neck, mouse incisors, crab carapace), the *movement* of tree foliage (palm frond nodding, aspen quivering, silver birch shimmering), the *colour* of minerals (amethyst, malachite, rhodocrosite), different *qualities* of sweetness (beet, cane, acacia honey, saccharine), the *gestures* of clouds (anvil, cirrus, strata, cumulus); and on the other hand through the child's direct experience in lessons (movements in eurythmy, timber grains in woodwork, rhythms in music, subtleties of shadow colour in stage lighting, nuances of voice pitch in foreign languages . . .).

The third phase in sensory education arrives when one engages the child's penetrative thinking to accompany the maturing and consciously awakening sense activity so that *insight* into the world can be arrived at. As detailed as possible a sense-registering of all aspects of the phenomena is required for this. It is what Goethe achieved par excellence in his 'discovery' of the archetypal plant, in his Newtonian-refuting colour theory and in other spheres of natural science. After pivotal experiences on his Italian tour he spoke of developing a *new way of seeing*. Thus a schooling in scientific method reaching beyond an instrument-measurable, purely quantitative empiricism can well be considered part of the aim of Waldorf's holistic approach to the senses.

The other bodily aspect that is acutely central to education is, of course, *the brain*. Neurologically, the senses play a big part in this, as do the child's acquisition of human movement and speech. On the other hand, the young brain, despite its size, has not arrived at the end of the road—ready for adult use. Joseph Chiltern Pearce in his *Evolution's End* and elsewhere, was one amongst others who drew attention to the far-reaching implications of current neurological research, particularly in the 1980s, into the character of the right and left hemispheres of the brain. This, for my understanding, explains why Steiner education is so successful academically while very specifically avoiding the long-term academically orientated approach to education which is mostly found in mainstream and, if one enquires into the *core* curriculum, also in specialized academies, choir schools, faith schools and the like.

For Steiner, the arts were vital in this respect—that is, those arts that came to expression through *colour* (painting and the child's illustration of narratives or written accounts), *form* (principally in form drawing and in three-dimensional modelling and wood carving), *tone* (experienced in eurythmic movement, singing which abounds in the Waldorf day, and recorder or other instrumental playing). While he rated these arts extremely highly in the earlier part of the child's school career—and it was a matter of being *engaged* creatively, not just copying a drawing, say, that the teacher had done on the board, which, however beautiful, stunts the child's own imagination—as far as I know he did not speak of their neurological significance. Yet it is quite clear that such artistic activities (choral recitation of poetry, creative writing and the performing of smaller plays, too) develop the imagination-connected right hemisphere alongside the plethora of left brain activities in the curriculum. In terms of the research referred to, this would ensure that the right-brain cells are well myelinated when it comes to the pubescent 'clean up' at the transition from the second to the third septennial phases; and this, in turn, due to the interaction of and mutual stimulation of the two hemispheres, means that the left side of the brain (on which academia mainly draws) benefits considerably. The Bonn research into Waldorf provision, published long ago in *Der Spiegel* on 14 December 1981, substantiates this to a marked degree.

Almost inexplicably in our logical age, these two bodies of complementary research do not appear to have made any significant impact on artistically impoverished approaches to education prevalent throughout the world. As far as I am aware, no longitudinal research has been undertaken to show how the resultant mental flexibility, imaginative insight, aesthetic perception, presence of mind and similar right-brain-related qualities survive the other-wise sclerotic advance in the mental capacities, which sadly often reach their climax in the aged. But I would not want this to detract from the main thrust of the bodily advan-tages (particularly in the region of the nerve-senses) of the Waldorf approach.

The child's inner energies/life forces and their nurturing in education

One of the surest, though not necessarily the most pleasant ways of appreciating the presence of a separate entity to the physical body in the human is to think of the state of the latter at death. After death, the life forces that have sustained the physical body through life both night and day are absent in the corpse. These life forces belong to and largely comprise what Steiner referred to also as a 'body', the *ether body*. How education nurtures the nature of the child is therefore the second part of the teacher's concern. Hallmarks of the etheric nature are *habit* and *rhythm*. The corpse, which is unsustained by the life processes, lacks rhythm. In the living body, even in sleep or other unconscious or semi-conscious conditions, rhythmic processes abound—not only the obvious respiratory and circulatory rhythms, but those of the digestion, cell regeneration, catabolism/anabolism and the like.

Steiner held that the life of pure habit was almost as deeply seated as these rhythmic processes. Education is directly reliant on habit when it comes to engaging (and retaining) the child's interest. Is the interest of the child easily roused? Or comparatively difficult? Is the interest of the child in what the teacher is bringing easy to retain or does it quickly subside or flit off towards something else. As a pedagogical task in helping the human being take hold of the life of habit (seated in the etheric nature), Steiner commended a revisiting of the medieval concept—indeed, something derived from much earlier times—of the four temperaments: sanguinity, choler, melancholy, phlegma.★ The interest of the first two is quickly roused, though the sanguine's interest can as quickly be diverted. The interest of the second two temperaments is gained only with effort, but once there (in the case of the melancholic) remains, while the phlegmatic's interest, as a rule, cannot compete so easily with its (less conscious but nevertheless strongly engaging) involvement in the inner processes of the ether body. Thus the teaching method, while it is both initially and subsequently utterly dependent on interest in the subject (if *learning* as well as teaching is going to happen!), at the same time has the opportunity of beneficially influencing each child individually to become master of one facet of its habitual nature—with potential repercussions on other facets.

Still deeper than habit in human nature are the rhythms of

★ For further characterizations of the four temperaments, their connection with certain topics, and their broadly therapeutic treatment in support of the child's developing personality in Steiner's approach to education, see pp. 80f, 84f, 121, 163 et seg., 183ff, 192, 202.

the ether body. These are very obviously influenced by the family's regular or irregular lifestyles, such as hours of sleep and times of meals, nearly all of which are beyond the school's jurisdiction—though the difference between residential and day schools in these respects is self-evident. However, education may be permeated through and through with rhythm, thus offering direct support for the ether body—always provided that the rhythms incorporated in the education are in harmony with the child's etheric nature.

From the outset, Steiner inaugurated the 28-day main-lesson of Lower and Upper Schools, in which one topic was concentrated on, e.g. *area* in mathematics or the *Reformation* in history. In the flow of tides, in the movement of sap in the plant and in similar phenomena in nature, this 28-day (lunar) rhythm is evident. Thus the individuality of each child, at the beginning of each school day—the main-lesson lasted two hours—was connected with one of the major life force principles of the solar system. Lessons in the rest of the day followed a weekly rhythm, well known to other educational and higher educational praxis. However, during each day, the *positioning* of each subject was not arbitrary but rhythmically supported the energies of the ether body, with, broadly speaking, artistic subjects following main-lesson (i.e. in the middle of the school day) and crafts and other more active subjects coming last on the timetable.

At the end of each main-lesson period—or simply once each lunar month if teachers begin their 28-day rhythms at different times—there was a so-called monthly festival (*Monatsfeier*) in which classes were all assembled and performed for one another, and at the following weekend for the parent body. The items demonstrated what lessons they had been involved in. These were not performances in any 'performing arts' sense, yet they made publicly visible what was being learnt—a vital part of the process in a Steiner school, which either obviates the need for, or emphatically takes educational precedence over what in other forms of education is referred to as *assessment*. At the same time they had a consolidating effect, assigning what had been learnt to those layers of memory from where it could later be fished from the depths, built on further, transformed or simply recalled—without, of course, any emphasis being placed in a highly competitive way on the last of these (i.e. in the form of tests/exams), which would tend to jeopardize the potential for transformation.

In some ways, still more profoundly and intimately connected with the teacher's methodology than the foregoing, is the use of the most cosmic of all rhythms, day and night—a use guaranteed through the main-lesson, which is another reason for its positioning at the beginning of each school day when the pupils are closest to coming out of sleep (some, especially in adolescence, are not nearly far enough out of it when they arrive at school!). Thus, before proceeding to a new topic—phosphorus following sulphur, say, in chemistry; dicotyledons following monocotyledons in botany; the precession of the equinoxes and its associated Platonic Year following the earth's revolution in astronomy; and so on—the topic of the previous day is remembered, reflected upon, looked at perhaps from one or two different angles, etc. And with the introduction of the new topic, a further support for the life forces becomes possible—what Steiner referred to as 'teaching the child to breathe'. Of course he meant that through *soul*-breathing in the lesson a healthy knock-on effect can be brought to bear on the rhythmical regularity and depth of the respiratory system itself. Examples of pedagogical devices that achieve this are:

(i)   when a theoretical fact that has been presented is followed by an illustration of it from real life;

(ii)   when some minutes in the teacher's presentation
requiring concentrated listening are followed by a par-
enthetic dialogue between teacher and a few pupils;

(iii) when a more serious aspect of the subject is followed by
a quick injection of humour;

(iv)   when the in-breathing of the soul in anxiety, sorrow or
apprehension is followed by its release in joy or relief.

In such ways—and one could further illustrate the principle by going into the kind of gymnastics taught, the spectrum of crafts selected, the way things such as grammatical
rules or number bonds are introduced to children in the
second septennial phase—education has the opportunity to
impinge on the life forces supportively, which can have an
enduring effect in one way or another throughout life.

Addressing, schooling and balancing the child's intelligences

While a child's psyche contains all three components
enjoyed by the adult—cognitional, emotional and
manual—it is self-evident, as is the undeveloped body at
birth, that there is still a long way to go before maturation
and full psychological growth are attained. In fact, in that
the physiological components manifest themselves less
visibly than the physical, their development in childhood is
by no means the end of the story. We might still find ourselves struggling with control of thought at the time of
menopause, or on occasion emotionally too easily swayed
in our twenties or thirties, or temporarily lacking completely disciplined will-power, for one reason or another,
any day of life. The quayside of childhood, however, offers

the teacher daily opportunities to help trim the sails of thinking, feeling and willing before the individual sets sail on the fully responsible voyage of life. How did Steiner see and cater for this?

Firstly he recommended an unwavering concentration on the *three soul forces* (as he frequently referred to them) during each septennial phase: 0–7 years an experiential (will) accent; 7–14 years an artistic (feeling) accent; and 14+ years a perceptively understanding (through thinking) accent. *Intuitive learning*, an *inspired discovery* of the wonders of the world, and an *awakening understanding* of the rationality of life imaginatively enlivened rather than narrowly confined also characterize the schooling of the three phases. 'Accent', however, does not mean monopolization. Experiential, strictly 'nonverbal' learning in the first septennial phase implies that the educator trusts implicitly on the long-term benefit (for feeling and thinking) to be derived from a thorough, devoted, consistent and morally sound engaging of the will. In the second septennial phase the education of emotional intelligence informs the will (flowing, as it were, from the past) as well as setting up the reservoir of schooled feeling which can be drawn on to pervade the awakening cognitional faculties. And thirdly, a logical solution to a problem (at 14+) needs to be both practicable and sensitive to all concerned if it is going to be of service.

But apart from these accents in Kindergarten, Lower School and Upper School, we have seen that each day was served with a threefold accent of subjects: more cognitive ones in main-lesson; in the middle of the school day, cultivating and enhancing artistic/aesthetic qualities immediately after main-lesson; and exercising predominantly the limbs for the last third of the day, often a double lesson in the afternoon—games, gardening or woodwork, for example. All of which, once more, offers endlessly creative scope for the pedagogue.

Further, each lesson can be viewed from a threefold point of view—taught in a threefold mode. The singing lesson, to take an example, can be structured so that in the learning of a new piece the rational intelligence can be drawn on in reading musical notation, and from Class 6 onwards a knowledge of the rudiments of music is built up—key signatures and key modulations, musical form, features such as sequence, accompaniment figures and so on. Not that this will be the first aspect of the song that the children will meet: the teacher's essentially non-musical introduction to it ensures that the *whole* child is addressed, first and foremost, through the 'story' contained in or implied by the poet's verses, and thereafter by some biographical anecdotes concerning poet, composer or arranger, perhaps, or allusions to the song's setting in cultural history. Of course, in an art such as music, opportunities for addressing the emotional intelligence may well pervade the whole lesson. It would be odd if this were not the case. These will occur particularly at the beginning of the lesson when singing a song that helps the soul connect with and expand into the prevailing season or that subtly touches on the stage of development that the pupils are going through, and also when entering deeply into those musical nuances that make a song part of humanity's cultural heritage and therefore educationally worth committing to memory. The third stage—harnessing the will forces—is arrived at when either the former stage reaches its climax and the song is prepared, say, for 'performance' in a festival or concert or when songs learnt by heart earlier in the year (or years) are sung through for sheer revival pleasure.

The foregoing is not to imply that each stage is strictly cordoned off from the other two, but clear emphasis on each will ensure that the child's threefold soul nature has been nurtured in a balanced way. Thus, by the end of the pupils' school career—with an important musical milestone having been reached before entry into Class 9—they will have achieved a fair, knowledgeable, practical and sensitive relationship to music, with an ever-deepening understanding of musical style and thereby potential insights into the ever-evolving consciousness of humanity from which *style* in all spheres of life derives.

The above example focuses on a lesson concerned primarily with one of the performing arts. Obviously the emphasis in mathematics lessons or metalwork will lie elsewhere in the soul's threefoldness. But through the structure of the day, thinking, feeling and willing will be schooled in an integrated way. The operative word is 'integrated', for a healthy lifestyle will depend on each person being in a position to exercise all three soul-intelligences. Childhood, being the precursor to this, is thus a rich opportunity for preparing for life, through an extensive (3 × 7 years), structured (three sections in the timetable each day) and infinitely flexible and creative schooling (the teacher's pedagogical skill at each moment in the lesson) of the three soul forces.

The self (or ego)

This brings us to the fourth member of the child: the self or ego.★ What are the opportunities during the school years that lend themselves to the appropriate strengthening of that

---

★ The text here and in subsequent passages elaborates Steiner's concept of the human ego, which does not necessarily have the overtones and implications of the term's use in other schools of thought.

component in the human make-up whereby human beings (eventually as adults) sift what is coming towards them from the outside, take note of the impulses engendered from within and thence *direct their own lives?*

For the pedagogue, the first thing to note is that the ego in childhood does not manifest in parallel with the seven-year phases of bodily development, soul phases and stages of consciousness. Its *independence*, the unique property of the human kingdom, thus makes itself felt from the beginning. The incision of the ego experience during the first three years, voiced when the child first uses the word 'I', comes immediately to mind as the unique expression of this in each person's biography. Common ego phenomena in child development are:

(i)   the so-called 'terrible twos' behaviour which is an exhibition (!) of often cussèd childhood obstinacy;

(ii) the Rubicon of the 9th/10th year;[*]

(iii) the conflict arising throughout the adolescent years, in varying degrees of intensity, of the teenager wanting to 'strike out' and the parent attempting wisely (or maybe at times failing miserably and unwisely!) to attain an authoritative position of diminishing yet still valuable guidance.

These humps in the road of child development, which are connected with this youngest yet hope-embodying member of our constitution, call for extra alertness and tact on behalf of the adult carer.

Being the most 'spiritual' member of the human being, the ego and its development in childhood, particularly its

---

[*] For fuller explanation of this nodal point in the child's development see pp. 91, 93f, 125, 158, 201, 239.

inherent independence, presents the most sensitive of tasks for the educationist. All brands of totalitarianism aim to thrash every trace of independence out of life, be it through propaganda, a culture of fear, the concentration camp or through other more subtle and insidious means. At the other extreme, leave the ego entirely untouched by education— and therefore also all sense of *morality* with which it is intricately connected—and you risk lumbering society with rampant crime and a culture (or *non*-culture) which drifts towards anarchy.

Steiner's contention was that the ego, in its highest sense, is a positive spiritual force/energy, but in keeping with the principle of human freedom it is open to degradation and corruption, whereby it gives itself over, as it were, to its lowest nature. Self-respect and self-awareness are as vital as respect for and awareness of others and the environment. Consciousness, be it in pictorial form or otherwise, of the integrity of the higher ego in humans (a power of self-guidance) can be enhanced through stories—mythological, allegorical, fictional or real. The lively telling of these genres forms a central part of Waldorf methodology. Such stories present the child in age-related ways with suitable role models via both heroes (to emulate) and villains of the piece (to deplore). Such enhancement is essential alongside those elements in education which empower the self, e.g. the training of scientific insight (as distinct from the mere learning of scientific 'facts'), or the acquisition of computer programming skills (as distinct from the mere efficient use of its facilities), or the cultivation of literary style, both its use and appreciation (as distinct from the mere decoding of meaning) and so on.

Such qualities/skills depend on what Steiner understood as the *age-relatedness* of the various subjects taught. Age-relatedness is intimately connected with the incarnation, development and responsible sensitivity of the ego. Ego energies can be crushed and filtered out of the child's condition by forced prematurity. Steiner's non-negotiable approach to 'formal learning' and especially his ideas about the appropriate introduction to literacy—I emphasize once more—come to mind. But the principle remains throughout the school: force the learning of something prematurely and we are liable to stunt those very qualities that we are seeking to engender. Equally—though possibly less obviously in our modern age and its headlong rush into adulthood—if certain faculties in the child are left fallow the likely result will be weaknesses.

The Waldorf maxim of emphasizing the importance of learning the multiplication tables in an *analytical* form right from the beginning of Class 1 is one of the most striking examples. So much of the Class 1 curriculum is presented as a synthesis and remains as such as far as the lessons are concerned. In arithmetic, however, Steiner pointed out that we have a golden opportunity—albeit in the most simple way—of exercising the child's analytical faculty if the tables are said (and of course then thought of) as the *product* being broken down into its *factors*. Or to give an example in child-speak: $3 = 1 \times 3, 6 = 2 \times 3, 9 = 3 \times 3$, etc. Once this format of the multiplication table is firmly established of course, i.e. known by heart by each individual in the class, flexibility of mind can be cultivated by juggling the numbers around. Here are two examples: 'a third of 36 is 12' (when fractions are on the agenda in Class 4), and '$33\frac{1}{3}$% of 27 is 9' (in Class 6 when percentages, ratio and suchlike mathematical topics form part of the curriculum). Education, seen in this way, could be said to consist of a long sequence of *unspoken messages* which the maturing ego can 'hear' and take respective account of on its journey towards a strong and responsible adulthood. Indeed, this is perhaps the most important task of all allotted to the educationist, if civilization is going to assist the future and uncover and awaken new capacities that will become necessary if that future is going to be *progressive*.

'Progressive'! What does that imply? More and more nations gradually acquiring nuclear weapons? More and more power to the economically 'developed' countries to subdue and control the rest of the world? More widespread longevity as the result of medical knowledge and the accompanying wherewithal to enjoy longer retirement? Everyone could devise their particular utopia no doubt. For Steiner, who was amongst the first to acknowledge the unprecedented advance in research and knowledge of the material world that characterized his time, the progress of humanity at this level necessitated a complementary advance in metaphysical insight. It might be put in the following way. The exoteric and the esoteric had got out of step, and the time had come to try and rectify this, if matter-oriented research and its derivative knowledge were not to plunge humanity into ever-engrossing depths of materialism.

★   ★   ★

Rather than decry the material advances that have revolutionized civilization over the past centuries we should look at where we are going, and it will be well if we trace—perhaps more consciously than we are wont—the historic background to the advance of physically confined scientific knowledge at the expense of the corresponding spiritual dimension to that advance. To do this thoroughly is well beyond the scope of an educational study such as this. I shall therefore confine myself to a brief yet significant summary of the origins of the situation. These, according to Steiner's research, pivoted crucially on AD 869, when the notion of 'spirit' was renounced by the Church at the Council of Constantinople. Among other historical studies is an article by A.P. Shepherd, 'The Battle for the Spirit' (published in the *Golden Blade*, 1963), where it is demonstrated how the events leading up to and stemming from that Council split eastern and western Christianity. As a symptom of that split, he cites how the latter became fertile ground for the advance of empirical science, as already hinted at, and points out, for those with artistic insight, the contrast between the eastern *icon* (a two-dimensional, non-representational 'imagination') and western art which led, even in religious painting and sculpture, over a number of centuries to the *physically representational*.

Though it seems a far cry from the first decade of the third millennium, the pope immediately preceding that Council was Nicholas I (his papal term of office being 858–67). Another student of this crucial turning point in the history of the West, Thomas Meyer (in his *Light for the New Millennium*), shows how it was Pope Nicholas who prepared the ground for the split and suggests that his superior consciousness sensed that without it the West would not have been able to develop freedom from the spirit (a) to enable a non-spiritual paradigm to investigate and harness the forces contained in physical matter; and (b) to permit, through that freedom from the spirit, the application of those harnessed forces for good or ill. Canon Shepherd concludes his article by quoting an 'Oxford theologian at a Convocation debate [as saying]: "Theologians are beginning to turn away from the Western idea of twofold man, back to the Eastern idea of man as spirit, soul and body."' Rudolf Steiner went much further, applying the necessity of returning to a *reinstatement of the spirit* to all walks of life, not merely to theological debate. From

Pope Nicholas to the century in which Steiner regarded materialism as having reached its peak (the nineteenth century) was a thousand years. During the catastrophe of the First World War (a devastating fruit of that materialism) Steiner insisted that there was no time now for theological debate before humanity's pressing need for *action*—which is not to demote any value in such debate that theologians might find rewarding. The founding of the first Waldorf School, it transpired in 1919, was one such form of action.

It was in the final stage of preparing for a lecture in which I wished to include a similar glance at this time span (from Pope Nicholas and the split of East and West to 1919) that I thought to look up Nicholas in a reference work. The entry ended with 'His Feast Day is on November 13'. I am not a person who is 'into' synchronicity, but a slight chill went down my spine—or was it a thrill?—when I realized that the day scheduled for the lecture was 14 November and that my thread of thought therefore was being spun (it being the evening before) precisely on Nicholas' Feast Day!

At this point, as stated earlier, we shall move on from having considered the nature of the child from a spiritually scientific point of view to how Steiner saw the role—and nature, too—of the teacher, using the opportunity to reflect that role through some of the author's personal experiences in a variety of capacities, all connected with Waldorf education.

THE TEACHER:
A FIFTH COMPONENT IN
EDUCATION THEORY*

*The author first proposed this in his doctoral thesis *An Appraisal of Steinerian Theory and Waldorf Praxis: How do They Compare?* University of Surrey (Roehampton) 1997.

2. A Curtain Raiser: Multiple Intelligences

Intellectualism and Education—The Age of Formal
Schooling—The Teacher's Rhetoric—Symptomatic
History—Crime—Pisa Research

'Just imagine it . . .'
The event which I have had reason to recall on numerous
occasions did not take place in the classroom. We had a guest
staying with us, a boy of 15 on exchange from a Waldorf
school abroad. As his period of stay included some holiday
time, I arranged some visits to London—Waldorf-inspired
sightseeing, from one point of view. On the occasion in
question, the inspiration came towards us from without
rather than from within.

We were in a long queue awaiting entrance to the Tower
of London, where the public was being admitted in large but
manageable parties of about 30, ready to be conducted round
the historic monument by a fully and formally uniformed
Yeoman of the Guard. As the turnstiles clicked, our party was
welcomed by one such of medium height, with ruddy
complexion and almost cerulean blue eyes that gazed with an
unusual mixture of engagement (considering he must have
seen it all a thousand times before) and active patience. We
were soon on our way, stopping at the first port of call,
where, true to type, our guide pointed out the four or five
main points of historic interest: that window overhead on the
inside of which such and such happened in 14-whatever-it-
was, an archway on the left through which . . ., a gateway on
the right leading to the Thames . . ., a scar in the masonry
which had occurred when . . ., and so on with each event

backed up with an exact date—interesting information by which you feel you are getting your money's worth, and after which you expect to be moved on to the next stopping point.

But not a bit of it! After he had gone through the standard drill, our Yeoman's style abruptly changed. He flung out an arm, fingers outstretched, and fixed the crowd with a penetrating look. With eyebrows dramatically skewhiffed, he lowered his Irish voice in a mood of stage-whispered confidentiality, hunched his shoulders and with a faint touch of threat said: 'Imagine it, Ladies and Gentlemen, imagine it!' His fantasy now at full play, he then went skilfully on, like a sheep dog rounding up the straggling sheep—the historically date-immersed minds of his intellectually-endowed listeners—until we were all gathered into the colourful flock of the details with which he described a particular event. As he did so, our minds erased centuries while the grey stones of the Tower yielded up the lovelost past, bringing life-size evidence, as it were, to his word-painting.

As other visitors sensed that here was a rare rhetorically virtuosic phenomenon, his crowd of 30 grew, like iron filings bunching round the pole of a magnet. I was as riveted as the rest, but distinctly remember thinking (in another layer of my consciousness) that this must have been the sort of thing that Steiner had in mind when he recommended a pedagogical technique for history lessons—to start with a summary of actual events with names, place, time, etc. and then change gear (my expression, not his!) and embark on a *vividly descriptive mode* of the historic episode. Add to this the advice to select those events which are *symptomatic* of a particular time, and you have the opportunity of conveying to the pupils a comparatively enduring, yet pictorially alive memory—floats in a pageant of history, upon or in between which it will be possible to place future encounters.

★ ★ ★

For over a century, much in education has plummeted lemming-like over the precipice of *intellectualism*, to the detriment of emotional and other intelligences. So much so that it is becoming increasingly difficult to distinguish between real intelligence and the ubiquitous mask of sharp intellect through which the genuine cognitional voices we need in our modern age get little opportunity to speak and be heard. As with many things there are anomalies where the left and right hands seem strangers to one another. For example, for some two years Ofsted has been applauding the scheme which aims at developing social, emotional and behavioural skills (SEBS). Yet in the same moment we are confronted with the expectation of the National Association of Able Children in Education—and we can leave aside the denigrating implication that if you aren't an Able Child then you aren't *able*—to appoint a 'lead teacher' to spot 'gifted children'. One example given was to get Year 2 children—a prime age for unadulterated SEBS-type pedagogy—to intellectualize over: 'If you were a dragon, who would you kidnap and why?'

The fairly recent (2003) Pisa research is a case in point. Finland's superior education (even in academic terms) was considered by the researchers to be partly but significantly due to the State's abiding by the long tradition of formal schooling beginning only at the conclusion of the first septennial period—something also maintained by Waldorf education, and one of Steiner's non-negotiables.

Other countries over the years had also followed the same tradition, Germany included. And yet, recent news from the latter discloses the fact that despite Germany's very long history of being a leader in culture on several levels and upholding high educational principles, and *despite the findings of the Pisa research*, the government has lowered the age of school entry.

This trend amongst one of the traditionally most thinking of European peoples is a serious 'sign of the times'. It seems to indicate that intellectualism has taken a firm hold of modern thought-forms to the extent that it either blinds those responsible to the importance of other forms of intelligence or possibly, through doubt persisting even in the face of research, filtering into emotional intelligence with the result that the latter succumbs to the pressure of a force approaching intellectual hysteria—a kind of emotional-intelligence suicide. And that is not even to mention those deeper recesses of intelligence that are associated with personal morality and ethical lifestyles. It was, of course, the role of the General Teaching Council to take the disciplinary action that led to the banning of the teacher who emailed confidential exam questions for Key Stage 3 to friends (2007). At the same time, without being judgemental, one cannot help wondering (a) what the education she received contributed (or failed to contribute) to her personal moral standards; and (b) how she might have taught in an educational ethos relieved of the kind of pressure that drove her to act in such a way that resulted in her being dismissed.

Not that it is all black and white. On the first day of March 2007, published league tables for London schools showed the Yesoday Hatorah Secondary School in Stamford Hill as coming first in the league. Rabbi Pinter, the head, was quoted as saying that he'd have preferred the school 'to have come second. Because then we'd have still have something to strive for'! The remarkably high exam success rate also quoted made it sound as though *that* was the purpose of the school's striving, with one interviewer (David Cohen of the *Evening Standard*) leaving the English exam results as a last taste. Yet the school rates moral standards so highly that none of its students go on to university because 'no campus in this country [is] morally acceptable'. The Rabbi insisted that the school's achievement was because there is 'no sex education . . . and [no] internet . . . [and] those sorts of distractions'. The journalist called it a 'curious world'. It cannot, of course, be paralleled with Waldorf except in so far as the young human being (and therefore life in the school) is seen as being altogether different from a mini-adult *in order* to produce the adult of the future. Curious it may seem, perhaps, but that's the way it is if one takes not the Rabbi's point of view, but the *developmental* approach to children's upbringing.

★   ★   ★

One wonders how many eminent thinkers will be needed to get the common-sense message across of the vital importance of taking active note of, preserving, nurturing and valuing childhood—indeed, treasuring both the 'early years' and those that follow that take the child to the threshold of youth. One thing is plain: we do not need Yeomen of the Guard to prod us into *imagining* the price we are paying for educationally neglecting the whole child. Daily the headlines spew their outpourings of terrorist bombing, paedophiles, knife amnesties, teacher absenteeism, university internet-plagiarism, corruption, broken homes, drug abuse, creativity-annihilating surveillance of education, fraud, the constant penalizing of the underprivileged, the swilling of culture into the gutters of society, the steep-curved increase in litigation 'revenge', child obesity, the commercial sexualization of the young, teenage pregnancies, video-game imprisonment of the mind, mortgage-fettered budgets and the like. One of the latest symptoms, prior to going to press (June 2007), was the consigning of the humble pencil sharpener to the weapons ban and the permitting only of sharpeners with tamper-proof blades. The story broke, moreover, just a few days after head teachers had been calling for staff, who were empowered to search pupils for weapons, to be equipped with 'stab-proof vests'. One could go on.

But how little do we stop to think that those suicide bombers, those paedophiles, absentee teachers, net-plagiarists, drug abusers, house-breakers and so on ad infinitum were once innocent babes in arms. Judges, it was reported, have been urged to avoid giving custodial sentences because the prisons are full to overcrowding. But our criminals, thieves, fraudsters, malingerers and perpetrators of the get-away-with-it attitude to life have one thing in common: they all received education. Between being born as that innocent babe and deliberately diverting money into his own pocket that could have benefited a charity, he went to school and received an education. It is not that education is the only means of restoring wholesomeness to all the various walks of life indicated by the above (though it would be more than 'a good start'). Nor is it that something lacking in education is some inexorable force behind the behavioural problems with which the globe is riddled (though, again, focused research in this direction is surely overdue).

Insight into what is truly educational does, of course, flash forth here and there. From the 2007 annual conference of the National Association of Head Teachers (NAHT) came the harsh signal that the State system was heading towards 'curriculum meltdown'. From a Waldorf standpoint, however, the warning seemed to be based more on the insufficiency of staff and resources than on an enquiry into the deeper educational implications of the curriculum. The General Secretary came a step closer to substance when commenting on the incursion into the system that stipulated that vocational training should start with 10-year-olds: Britain was in danger of producing 'an army of the unemployable'. A step closer, perhaps, but hardly in itself a vision of what skills, creative forces and values need to be educationally nurtured in readiness for the uncertain future we all face.

A starting point would be the Yeoman getting through with 'Imagine it, Minister, the kind of education our children receive needs urgently looking into, in all its minutiae and repercussions'—getting through and doubling, trebling, quadrupling the audience who hear his message and *act on it* positively.

3. The Ego's 'Three Sheaths'

Waldorf at the Equator—The Induction of the First Waldorf Teachers—Speech, Music, Modelling—Steiner's Teaching Experience—Accreditation

'Clouds of Rain . . .'
I had just lit the candle in my tiny room and had begun sorting out my luggage. Night had fallen suddenly as it does at the equator. A fanfare of sunset as wide as the sky blazed as the day faded, after which it was as if a shutter quite suddenly dropped down, leaving you on a moonless night drenched in the warm darkness below, with star-studs overhead spelling awe and majesty on the cosmic memory pad. Weary from travel it was not long before I sought the comfort of soft pillows beneath the mosquito net. Then it was that the intense silence of nature was broken. Broken is too harsh a word. It was not the cry of a hyena from the adjacent safari park or the bark of a suspicion-roused dog roaming the campus. It was the sweetest sound of children's voices, touching the night air as gently as the scent of white jasmine.

The song came from the next room, a small dormitory of boys, the proximity of which I must have been told about when being introduced to 'the geography'. But with all the impressions of a new country to take in, I had not earmarked the fact for special attention. The new sights and sounds were no more than daubs on the memory, waiting to be looked at and listened to with greater attention in the ensuing days. In this frame of mind, it took me some moments to disentangle, indeed disenchant, myself from the mood that all the circumstances evoked and register first *what* the song was and then that it was one I had written myself—both words and music! It was as unpretentious as the simplest of rounds could be (though the boys were not singing in parts), yet made a deep impression—especially here, not far from the African Rift Valley, and within a stone's throw of giraffe and rhino, a melody within the range of the fifth, born of childlike western consciousness, about as far removed as you could be from the surrounding culture of the predominant Masai tribes people and their ecological setting.

My visit was planned to coincide with the inauguration of a teacher training course for Kenyans, Ugandans and Tanzanians who were interested in becoming Waldorf teachers. Waldorf colleagues from Denmark and South Africa were the leading lights, but I was more than happy to 'sing along' as the invited guest and be responsible for some of the lectures and workshops. The instantaneously ignitable enthusiasm of the student teachers was an inspiration in itself.

The campus of the school where the training course was held was on the outskirts of Nairobi, three or four minutes from the town centre by helicopter (there must be a tang-tongued Masai equivalent for 'as the crow flies') but by road something to think twice about, with ruts, potholes and gullies pockmarking and lacerating the red-dirt surface in such a way that would reduce a brand new Mercedes into a bone-shaker in no time. The National Safari Park is fenced on three sides of a vast rectangle open to the west so that the game are free to forage away from the water holes when the rains come. It then becomes essential, of course, for the fence around your own property to be built as high as necessary to contain the wild life. The manager of the world famous Kitengela glass (an ex-Waldorf pupil and Trustee of the school), had taken an extra precaution. She had constructed a room for herself, perched some 8–10 feet high on a pillar above her property; looking somewhat like a water tower, there was a device for elevating her dogs into safety each night. And here in the most primitive cooking and sanitary conditions, Waldorf blossomed with the glowing colours of children's paintings on the classroom walls, with music and poetry sung and recited each day, with the utmost care taken to create the conditions appropriate to holding the Waldorf Children's, and Youth Sunday services, in one of the class-rooms decked for the occasion and so on.

★   ★   ★

It is instructive to compare the way Steiner prepared the first group of Waldorf teachers for the task during the late summer of 1919 and the advice he gave for teacher training five years later. The initial induction course consisted of three con-current and correlative series of lectures/workshops. In the fourteen lectures he looked at the nature of the human being, with some emphasis on childhood, not only from a psychosomatic but expressly from a spiritual-psychosomatic point of view. These lectures contained little reference to the classroom per se but bore out in exemplary fashion his contention that the whole of education be rooted in as deep as possible an understanding of the child's nature and the development of the human being through childhood. The second lecture course contained practical advice to teachers, focusing principally on pedagogical issues, advice that Steiner was in a strong position to give, not only because of his spiritually developed insight but also because he had accu-mulated much experience of teaching, even during his late teens. (Although this had not included *classes* of pupils, the experience included a wide range of subjects up to con-siderably advanced levels and, perhaps even more sig-nificantly, the education of a boy who had severe learning difficulties. Through devising appropriate pedagogical methods, Steiner was able to prepare the boy sufficiently to gain qualification as a medical doctor.) The third session each day had the mode of a workshop in which Steiner raised topics for discussion. So the teachers designate had the opportunity to build up their understanding to date of the nature of the child and their perception of the potentiality in various subjects to address the age and stage of development of the children they were about to teach and, from these two, devise appropriate pedagogy.

Was this a hypothetical situation, one of the major obstacles with which teacher training has to contend? Yes and no. *Yes*, in that there were no children actually present so that any validity-efficiency of the ideas put forward could be verified day by day. *No*, in that (a) 'childhood' came alive in such fullness through what Steiner brought that it was the next best thing; and (b) the feedback which their efforts and suggestions received from Steiner could enter straight away into didactic discussion. These three parallel courses— extended further in lectures when Steiner was visiting Stuttgart during the next five years—are still regarded by many Waldorf teachers as the bible of their calling.

Clearly, any bible is for study, either amongst a group or for each person in private. What about the maelstrom of daily life in the classroom, in the playground and in the school corridor? This is where the contrasting (might it be supple- mentary?) advice of summer 1924 comes into effect. Instead of taking 14 intensive days, it was more or less uttered in one short sentence: *Teacher training?* (if I paraphrase): *practise modelling, music and speech*. Fortunately Steiner lifted the veil which covered the far-reaching wisdom behind this *mot*. Had he not, we might have taken more decades spy-glassing the enigmatic clue he had in mind than those which we have spent putting the advice into practice—or left it fallow, ignoring or only half-heartedly following it, as the case may be. Or, worst of all, we could put undue trust in *written* assignments during teacher training, frequently the time-consuming price we pay for 'formal' accreditation. From this standpoint, and in view of the increase in extreme behavioural difficulties that are currently the cause of grave concern, it would be worthwhile reviewing (yet again) teacher training. It is there, after all, that those skills begin to be engendered that will be needed in the teacher's future career. A somewhat sobering comment follows.

At its 2007 annual conference the National Association of Head Teachers (NAHT) voiced resistance to providing alternative education for more than six day-exclusion pupils, lest the move led to soaring numbers of permanent exclusions. Waldorf schools are not unknown for pupil exclusions, but I firmly believe that the emphasis placed on understanding the child and the pedagogical praxis that results from this pre-empts the crossing of exclusion thresholds in by far the majority of cases.

It was all very well for someone with Steiner's advanced spiritual capacities to describe the complex nature of the child—that is, the human being in childhood. The physical body and its major development throughout the first 18 years of life is a subject in itself, even a special branch of professional medicine. A psychosomatic approach to education, where soul and body are seen to develop in tandem, must expect to discover equal complexity in the *psychological* journey of childhood. This, however, was not all. Steiner insisted on the spirit being an entity in its own right, not just an attribute of soul that could be knifed off as if it were some sort of acute metaphysical appendicitis, and the human being none the worse for wear.

Moreover, Steiner saw the spirit entity in the child, the incarnating ego and the self-consciousness by which it is experienced, not only as having two human 'organizations' into which to incarnate, but also a third: the element of *life*. It is self-evident that the physical is permeated with life forces (no longer the case with the corpse). In Steiner's approach to education, therefore, the teacher needs to take into account three *sheaths* (as he sometimes referred to them), which in themselves interpenetrate—the physical being the only sheath that consists of space-taking substance, so to speak.

We thus have the physical member of the human constitution for the teacher to take professionally into account and three metaphysical (non-physical) members. We can view this fourfold membering as the most spiritual member, *the ego or self, gradually incarnating during childhood into its three sheaths*, as if three soluble elements entered into a body of water, bringing about chemical changes relative to each one and to each's reaction on the others. To get on closer terms with this, it was Steiner's contention that the practice of speech, music and modelling would engender those forces in the teacher—or one might see it as releasing what is potentially there, but dormant in one degree or another—which would enable a 'perception', an appreciation, an understanding of the three metaphysical members in the child and their manifestation in the physical (i.e. sense-perceptible) to grow.

Hence we have *two professional approaches* to the teacher's task of understanding toddler, child and youth, and therefore of the art of education, as 'child'-related and metaphysically beneficial as the paediatrician's art of healing must be child-bodily sound. The beam of this understanding of all aspects of child nature can then be directed towards all aspects of education, whether it be teaching philosophy or economics to Class-twelvers (18 years), introducing vulgar fractions to 10-year-olds, narrating North American mythology to, say, the Seventh Class (13 years) or singing through the simplest of rounds which a visitor might casually hear as it wafts from a neighbouring dormitory while the magic of an equatorial night descends and sleep starts to claim the consciousness of a tired and contented group of Masai boys—loved by their teachers, certainly through the embrace of generous heart forces, but *also through an ever-deepening understanding* of what is happening in the 'equatorial magic' of childhood.

4. 'Secrets of the World Streaming Through in a Living Way'

Putting Steiner's Recommendations into Practice—Teacher
Training—Nature Stories—Nurturing Creative Inner
Faculties—Prescriptive Curricula

Warthog 2b

More from East Africa. The students were conferring in
huddles. They had been introduced to a genre of narrative
told already in Class 1 in a Waldorf school: the *nature story*. In
it, some natural object in the environment is described,
focusing on a particular detail which the teacher has chosen
because, to her, it epitomizes the quality, the energies, the
overall gesture of the object. There are two conditions. The
object in the story has to be taken from the immediate
environment where the children go to school, so that preferably they will have already experienced it before the story
is told; and the detail should not only be characteristic of the
object generally but representative of it *at the time of telling the
story*. It would be unusual to speak of a sunflower, say, while
it is still producing leaves around its light-seeking stem but
before there is any sign of the bud that is going to burst into
Van Gogh glory. Not that this would present a problem per
se, but there will be other events in the plant world at that
particular stage of the sunflower's growth that the children
should have their attention drawn towards if the story is
going to be an example of the genre that Rudolf Steiner
recommends.

The students concerned were participants in the first

Waldorf teacher training course to be held in that part of East Africa. On the doorstep the Savannah stretched as far as the eye could see, across to Nairobi on one side, the high risers looking like minute threads of blanket-stitch where sky met earth. On the other side the distant hills terminated a vista into which one knew the great African Rift Valley stretched north-south, opening up the earth like a deep scar, clawed by a hunting lioness on the flank of a donkey, all of cosmic proportions, in which stars still kept the secrets of time strictly to themselves.

With the majesty and awe of the very soul of Africa at our feet, it was now our turn to prey—not with ravenous fang but with sharpened observation. After some discussion we settled on two characteristic local phenomena. These were, as a somewhat humorous contrast, the movements of warthog and giraffe, with the latter stretching its periscope neck in order to nibble the tender shoots growing on the top of the umbrella-like acacia trees, and alongside this condescending aloofness the bouncy, snout-led strutting around of the warthog, tail erect, like the licked finger of someone in Harris Tweed plus fours and a deer-stalker held up to detect the exact direction of the wind. A contrast indeed: to the giraffe's towering frame, almost gliding effortlessly along, be it walking or galloping—there must be a delectable Masai word that depicts their lolloping gait—while several feet below her eye-lash glamour (further than you'd care to fall off a ladder while apple-gathering)—the warthog seems so earthbound that every effort to move its body seems like an award-winning triumph over gravity's relentless determination to curb all promenading that smacks of spirituality. Lofty superciliousness beside unapologetic pragma incarnate, as it were.

Significantly, no one asked for bibliographical references

or to hear written examples of a nature story read out (very unlikely in the replicated situation of a group, say, of London students). Their ignited imaginations leapt and crackled like flames from the burning bush as they embarked on the task of creativity with the *exact phenomenological observation* that was required, born, it seemed, of lifelong, savannah-soaked sense impressions. It was as if they immediately identified within themselves that quality which Steiner describes so eloquently in the course of his lectures entitled *The Essentials of Education*: '[T]eaching should not have its origin in anything we've learnt and then apply, but should originate from our being permeated by the secrets of the world streaming through us in a living way.'

★   ★   ★

A sunflower smiling and nodding complacently in late summer or a sweet-scented violet hiding its light under a bushel of leafy shyness, or a giraffe's agile lips manoeuvring their thorn-threatened way amongst the fresh, tender leaves of an acacia, or . . . These are not images that sound as though they contain the secrets of the universe, rather dwarflike, perhaps, beside birth and death, or the appearance of a hitherto unknown comet. But if a tiny mistletoe berry can be part of a cure for cancer (used in the well-known Iscador medicinal treatment) we should not be blind to the 'daisy at our feet', as Wordsworth put it, on seeing the glory of heaven in the most humble of natural wild flowers. Humans surely have it in them, if they can only find the way.

If—and only if—teachers could first find the means of identifying where the 'secrets of the world' are to be found, and secondly open the floodgates of consciousness, cultivate the multi-layers of human intelligence (instead of being stuck in the all too limited intelligence of the intellect), the increasingly prevalent and increasingly large curriculum studies coming on the market (leaden weight in the saddle of creativity) would become largely superfluous. They would certainly shrink back to the bare essentials that external inspectors appear to be unable to do without—though otherwise locked safely in some glass-fronted bookcase in the teachers' library gathering inter-inspection dust. To regard the curriculum as 'prescriptive', as one spokesperson of Waldorf education was quoted in the *Times Educational Supplement* (November 2003) as having said, would be unthinkable. One hardly expects the voice of the executioner to come from the ranks of the executive!

One direction leads into dry, didactic theory, the other into lively teaching. This is not to imply that Steiner's first set of lectures in 1919 is dry theory. Working with them in order to understand the nature of the child more deeply releases qualities in teachers when they are 'at the chalk face'. I had to think of that once in a public workshop in Israel when a long experienced teacher, who had seen the inception of the Kibbutz movement in the country, referred to the very early days when Jews started emigrating from different parts of the world. They had to build up infrastructure and get daily life going as quickly as possible, she pointed out, which meant putting their hands to all sorts of unaccustomed work. In the case of setting up schools it was a matter of 'cooking the teachers in six weeks'! Things have moved on now, of course.

★   ★   ★

In the Kenyan Rudolf Steiner School, Mbagathi, where the training course was taking place, we were not trying to emulate that, and certainly not Steiner's lightning 14-day induction course—even a tenth of his skills in that direction would have been welcome. But knowing that what we studied in the course would probably seep into classroom praxis once the participants got back to their neighbouring countries, we were trying to engender skills that didn't only remain 'in the head' like parched seeds waiting for the rains to come. Thus, each day, one or two groups would come to the front of the room, announce the title of their nature story and present it, either as a little drama with two or three characters speaking impromptu or with a narrator seated in story-telling fashion and the rest portrayed imaginatively in mime.

With 'The Giraffe and the Acacia Tree', for example, it was amusing to see the acacia tree fluttering her fingers like the acacia leaves in the breeze, fearful at the thought of the giraffe making a meal of them—fluttering fingers alternating with long index fingers (thorns) stiffly poking as the tree tried to ward off the hungry giraffe's persistent advances. The giraffe was standing on *two* chairs, legs slightly apart and arms stretched above the head for the long neck, while the folded hands nuzzled and nibbled among the thorns—not wolfing the tender shoots down ravenously but rather as if relishing something from the Delicatessen counter in Harrods.

Most of the titles were self-explanatory, consisting solely of the two 'creatures' (often an animal and a plant) who were the dramatis personae. Strangely enough, however, it is the less descriptive one—the odd man out—that sticks in the memory, perhaps because of the slightly humorous murmur of appreciation that rippled through the 'audience' on hearing the title rather dispassionately announced: 'Warthog 2b!' It sounds distinctly as if it were some bureaucratic missive destined for the filing cabinet, but believe me, it was an engaging nature story. Do feel free to try it out ... and good luck with the perpendicular tail as you simulate a warthog's movements while bouncing jauntily round the kitchen table!

5. Extrapolating Standard Education Theory from Steiner's Oeuvre

Teachers' Choir—Curriculum Petrifaction, Proliferation and Prescription—Charisma and Conceptualization—The Teacher's Heightened Consciousness—Sleeping, Dreaming, Waking—Birth of the Child Within—'Study of Man'

'It's snowing!'

True. I glanced over my shoulder almost as a reflex, and then continued conducting the Mozart we were preparing for the forthcoming celebration. But I had not reckoned on the difference that snowflakes softly cloaking the familiar school buildings as they drifted earthwards would have on conductor and choir. The former's baton went on wagging its four andante beats in a bar; the latter became convulsed in excitement, totally incompatible with the suave and hallowed mood of the motet they were singing, and drifted—quicker than the snowflakes that were coming down, it seemed—to watch the spectacle. I stood alone looking at their backs—a bunch of nose-pressed-to-window-pane captives!

Excitable 10-year-olds, you are probably thinking? Not a bit of it! The choir consisted of the entire teaching body of the Johannesburg Waldorf School (Michael Mount) who were rehearsing one of their items to mark the school's coming of age (1960–81). It took a moment for the penny to drop—a rather flake-drifting moment. Most of the teachers had never seen snow in their whole lives. Abroad, maybe in one or two cases—but certainly not alighting on their school.

The choir practice did eventually resume, but none of us was ever quite the same again. Snowy cosmic whiteness caressing the soul unexpectedly is not something to be swept away with the ease and efficiency of getting rid of slush on the streets of Zurich!

★   ★   ★

Rudolf Steiner (1861–1925), the inaugurator of Waldorf education (or possibly better named *Steiner* education, now that we are nearing 150 years since his birth), gave a fortnight's education course to the teachers designate of the first school (Stuttgart, August 1919). We will come to that, but I wish to approach it via an oft-quoted remark he made which encapsulates the essence of the education. 'At the Waldorf School'—it was so named, partly after the Waldorf-Astoria factory, the children of whose workforce attended—'we do not have programmes: we only have children and teachers!' Presumably Steiner had in mind *prescribed curricula*, in using the word 'programmes'—what today, more at higher educational level, would probably be referred to as modules. This is not to say that there was no curriculum at the Waldorf School. In fact, some little while after the school had been up and running, one of the foremost amongst its eminent class teachers gathered together what was being done, class by class, subject by subject, under the title *Lehrplann* (curriculum). She produced a fairly slim volume, which bears somewhat the same resemblance to a lesson in the school day as a map (plan) might bear to a journey—not so much of the *what*: turn to the left at the third set of traffic lights and after 3.5 miles take the right-hand fork etc., but the *how*, the *what was it like*, the account of what was confronted en route, the varying speeds, the significant landmarks, the more or the less attractive scenery. The experience of every journey is bound to be unique, not only for all journeymen, but for each time each journeyman makes the 'same' journey. Such an approach appears in stark contrast to the huge 'door-stoppers' that are more and more frequently being turned out as the Waldorf curriculum, either at the request of governmental authorities at national or local level or, one has to admit, at the behest of well-meaning educationists who have either misinterpreted or not understood the very obvious status which Steiner accorded the curriculum.

One can observe something similar happening in mainstream education. The theorists at higher educational level are preaching the value of looking at education from a logical and *fourfold* point of view (aims, the nature of the child, curriculum, pedagogy or method), while the legislators, who seal political debate into black and white, mostly boil everything down to the (National) curriculum. This at its worst precisely and prescriptively lumps the *what* with *how* to teach it, *how* to evaluate it. And the less successful participants of the evaluation schemes, which are made publicly competitive and so on, are named and shamed.

Small wonder that the parents, meanwhile, all too frequently find themselves as piggy-in-the-middle, scrambling for places. This year (2007) a mere 11.3% of appeals against the schools to which their children were allocated were successful. Margaret Morrissey, spokesperson for the National Confederation of Parent Teacher Associations (NCPTA), commented that the increasing fall in successful appeals was 'becoming more and more disturbing every year ... [in that] children's and young peoples' education ... is not progressing in the way that it should'. Not a glimmer of recognition that the fight for places is all based on the unquestioned supposition that the education on offer is what is appropriate for childhood.

Professor Alan Smithers of the University of Buckingham with his outspoken 'schools have been reduced to factories for producing test and exam scores' seems, in fact, to be identifying the fundamental flaw in the system as one of its main aims. Be that as it may, such 'hows' are as far from the art of pedagogy as an instructor's manual is from the art of sailing on the high seas. Whilst a thousand commentators, taking their cue from the Latin derivation of the word, have pointed out that education means 'to draw from', the practitioners, bent on quantitative value for money, insert their value-knowledge between the nature of the child and that which purports to 'draw from' that true nature. The appellation 'crammed' is falling into disuse, but cramming remains essentially what is going on through the process of imparting purely factual knowledge, followed by the testing of what can be recalled by the pupil (through whatever method). Nor is the resultant educational burden for the soul made any lighter by the opportunities now opened up of downloading (NB *DOWN ... LOADING*) from the web. (Will the notion of education being *uplifting* ever return?)

In demoting, or at least subduing, the status of the curriculum as he did, could Steiner have foreseen the danger of petrifying creative teaching? After the two weeks induction course, which concentrated mainly on the nature of the child and then to some extent on the creative faculties of the teacher (to bring about an *art* of education)—as diametrically opposite as could be to a programme accessible, say, through 'software'—*just* before school began, he outlined a very broad curriculum. It merely fleshed out somewhat those references to curriculum that had occurred during the initial training (*Ausbildung*), where it provided good examples for either meeting/addressing the nature of the child at each stage of development or for engendering pedagogical instinct in the teachers-to-be through their having to discuss the 'how'. The extensive Waldorf curriculum studies that are currently being published, of course, have their value, and one can admire the thought that has gone into them; but if they become door-stoppers in the sense of *preventing the opening of the door of creative teaching*, then their claim to be Waldorf comes seriously into question.

When the first Waldorf school had been going a couple of years, the task began of adding the Upper School classes (ages 15–18, a new class each year). At a meeting when the curriculum for these years was being discussed, Steiner, apparently without qualms, advised the omission of a certain subject as there was no one to teach it adequately. Again, it rings the same bell: no programmes; only teachers and children—and in this case 'teach what can be taught well, bearing in mind age-relatedness, rather than slavishly following a set curriculum'. This reflects pointedly how Steiner accorded the 'what' second place to the 'how' (in achieving the aim, the 'why'). Although the compartmentalizing of education theory has only become fashionable since Steiner's day, one could rephrase it in Waldorf terms into: *why* (aims), *who* (the nature of the child), *what* (curriculum), and *how* (pedagogy), with all components being subservient to, and so addressing, the nature of the child. Such an education affords the best chance of imparting to each individual what is needed as a self-directing force in modern life.

★   ★   ★

Of course, to achieve this all teachers have to be singing from the same song sheets (we shall return to Mozart by and by). I was once travelling to a young Waldorf school in East Anglia when I fell into conversation with an elderly man who expressed a deep interest in education and therefore in the forthcoming lecture on which my mind was particularly focused. It transpired that he had been school doctor at Summerhill in A.S. Neill's day, no less. The conversation revolved less around the remarkably incisive effect that the Summerhill approach had had on educational thought in general than on the comparison between Summerhill as it had been when Neill was at the helm and the recent bad press it had at that time been dragged through. I asked the doctor for his considered opinion, knowing full well how the truth can get distorted once a journalist gets on the scent of what might make a sensational article. His comments were very fair and helpful in restoring something of a true picture but I mention the whole incident here because of one particular remark. Opposite all his admiration for Neill he expressed the opinion that charisma on its own may succeed but could not be guaranteed to continue beyond the charismatic person's term of office. In his view, despite the writings we have, Neill was not able fully to *conceptualize* how he achieved his successful reputation.

When the late Professor Ted Wragg scathingly remarked on the heaped-on layers of directives coming from the Ministry in 2005 with 'every teacher, every school [is] in thrall, mind-slaves to the Prime Minister's office', he was, of course, denouncing the opposite scenario. It seems to me that both extremes—that inclining towards boundless teacher freedom and that of the mind-slaves and their task-masters—place insufficient emphasis on the true position of the teacher. A fifth component in education theory? Steiner did not actually teach at the Waldorf School, but there are plenty of anecdotes which show that he had a charismatic reputation among the pupils. Nevertheless, if one wants to explain why the Waldorf approach to education has not only persisted through influencing educational thought, but how it has grown into the largest independent *educational* movement in the world (independent of 'orthodox' influence), then one must turn to the way Steiner was able to conceptualize what after all was a very spiritual approach. He achieved this in terms that modern consciousness could relate to, grasp, work with, put into practice and—perhaps this is his greatest gift—*evolve* so that it could be adapted for considerably diverse cultures across the world as well as extended to tackle the very special needs and problems that have surfaced in mainstream education, which were either hardly or not at all evident in his day.

Perhaps the most widely known Waldorf principle that Steiner referred to and elucidated time and again is the significance of the *septennial phases of childhood*, 0–7, 7–14, 14–21, the three phases taking the child through youth to the very brink of adulthood. One perspective on this relates to the type of consciousness broadly characteristic of each phase. However active or vociferous the child is in the first seven years, the consciousness is one that is essentially *sleeping*. By degrees it passes through a *dreaming* state in the next seven years, finally entering the first decisive steps of *awakening* as the child passes through the gateway of puberty etc. Modern conditions often accelerate the phases, but the sequence will surely remain.

Self-dependence, though present to a minor extent all along, is for Steiner the hallmark of having outgrown the phases of childhood. Leaving the aims of education on one side, the self of the teacher directs its activity towards its professional task of understanding the nature of the child, of fathoming the value of a particular subject that will form part of the educational process, and of artistically shaping the methodology (pedagogy) by which the subject is taught into a creative experience for both pupils and teacher. Such a self-directed approach to the teacher's task can result in *imaginative insight* at the level of awaking consciousness, in *inspirational rapport* with the class at the (higher) level of quasi-dream consciousness, and in *innovative and incisive intuition* when confronted with situations throughout the teaching day which necessitate drawing on that level of consciousness that has been fructified by sleep.

This could be described as the teacher's professional way of interpreting and working with the saying from the Gospel: 'Except ye become as little children, ye shall not enter the kingdom of heaven.' The *birth of the child within* is not only symbolized in Christianity: we find it in the so-called Black Virgin of Chartres (pre-Christian), the 'child' Horus in Egyptian mythology, the god Mithras dear to many an ancient Roman soldier, and so on.

So if the choirmaster is suddenly left looking at empty seats while his sopranos, altos, tenors and basses are glued to the window like gleeful children during a freak fall of snow, he can at least gain comfort by conducting his thoughts towards the fact that there is more in his choristers than meets the ear: they all have a professional relationship to the cultivation of *the birth of the child within*. Every teacher can, after all, be likened to a snowflake with its sixfold symmetry. Three of the 'folds' are the heritage of the three states of child con-sciousness (sleeping, dreaming and waking). The other three are her efforts to consciously work with those states in her daily praxis—in the form of developing imagination, inspiration and intuition. Small wonder that so-called Steinerian education theory implies the addition of a *fifth* component—*the teacher*—to the academically orthodox four.

6. Initial Teacher Training and Ongoing Teacher Education

Teacher Training as a Transformative Process—Changing Times—Graduation—Collegiality—Faculty Meetings—The Teacher's Inner Life

'Would you like some butter?'
The noise level was on a par with that in an airport departure lounge. Much higher, if you limit your consideration to the noise created by the conversations taking place between human beings who, when awaiting announcements about flights, are seldom to be seen going at it hammer and tongs on some issue that has touched a nerve. Though thoroughly at home in the large gathering of some two hundred people—another contrast with the airport where you feel as small and insignificant as an aircraft 30,000 ft overhead, itself a mere speck beside a towering mass of white cumuli or against a backdrop of horizon-stretched colour—the intense conversations were bypassing me as if I had been a lone vehicle parked on the hard shoulder of a motorway during the rush-hour. The main reason for this was that the language of the conference was not my mother tongue, and whatever fluency I used to have had now acquired some ten years of rust through disuse.

So why feel at home rather than marginalized? It was a Waldorf teachers' conference. The energy was buoyant. In the company of those who share the deeper impulse of your life's task, you can 'identify'. Nevertheless, when someone at my table noticed my breakfast plate and offered me the butter in English, and in an English manner, it added an enormous personal touch. He was not a visitor to the region like myself but taught English as a foreign language in a Viennese Waldorf school.

★ ★ ★

My thoughts on the difference between impoliteness and simply the lack of politeness are not relevant here, but a word on colleagueship is in place. There was a short period in the early development of the first Waldorf school when clearly collegiality had broken down—I am going by the reports which appear in the so-called *Konferenzen*, the teachers' meetings which took place with Steiner present whenever it was possible for him to be in Stuttgart. The tone that comes across from the reports (since made available in both English and American publications) is much more severe than the incident would seem to warrant. One gathers that Steiner was making a point of the importance of collegial coopera- tion. It is my belief that, apart from the obvious—in the work place it is vital to pull together and create an atmosphere conducive to work—he had his eye on the future as much as, if not more than, the then present.

Steiner's knowledge on both planes, the spiritual and the earthly (or the scientific and the spiritually-scientific), was of great extent, and he had a deep understanding of humanity and human situations and dilemmas, too. Given a modicum of good will, it is difficult to imagine situations of conflict arising that he would have been unable to steer towards resolution. But it was more than that. Cooperative collegi- ality would be a prerequisite for the future when Steiner's knowledge and understanding—he was already 58 when the school was founded—would not be accessible directly through his presence. Faculty meetings would need to become the equivalent of a *research cluster* in which the Waldorf impulse could be carried forward into the decades and century yet to come. Times change. Children change. Teachers need to extend their appreciation and under-standing of such change and relate it to their professional pedagogical task. In some area or other, inner transformation will be called for in order to avoid getting stuck in the past. Transformation needs to be seen, where appropriate, publicly at the Waldorf level. However, it is even more important at the personal level, the latter being fundamental to the former, as is clearly the message to be gleaned from the fact that the many *professional meditations* that Steiner made available to teachers hardly ever explicitly refer to teaching but all focus on the personal development of the individual who carries the pedagogical responsibility.

Some years ago on a graduation occasion of the London Waldorf Teacher Training Seminar, a mature student who brought valuable life experience to the course, and who had become very deeply imbued with the Waldorf impulse and all that belonged to it, made an unforgettable remark (which will follow in due course). It had come to the point in the graduation proceedings at which both years had shown examples of their work in various subjects—eurythmy, singing, drama, speech, etc. But here it became evident that some of the best wine was kept till last. The 'mace', at this point in such ceremonies, is traditionally handed over to the second (final) year graduates. They, with adrenaline flowing and fantasy bubbling, reflect on the seminar training with hilarious caricatures (both visual and aural) of tutors' idio-syncrasies. All the fun of the fair is ushered in, which can make your sides ache with laugher, your soul expand with joy at the journey you've shared, and yet eyes here and there in the company well with tears at the thought of having to bid one another farewell as life paths diverge and the voice of individual destiny separates out from the chorus of the group.

Teacher training (*Ausbildung* in German) is not a lifelong journey as is ongoing teacher education (*Fortbildung*).★ The teacher education road continues for as long as the soles of your pedagogical shoes last (given, perhaps a bit of cobbling en route). Each student's life path has led to the training, which resembles the roundabout we all encircle together for two years before we head off on the first exit that looks promising. Perhaps encircling is not the ideal image. The inner process necessary in initial teacher training—change through insight, aspiration, knowledge and the way it is acquired and the development of pedagogical skills—is more like an upward-leading spiral. At the risk of pun-ishment, would *aspiraling* be worth coining to serve the purpose?

Or a common clothes peg may be preferred as a tangible metaphor for what happens in initial training. The two pieces of wood (or plastic) with which the peg is made represent the before and after—the karmic journey that led to the training and the karmic journey that follows after it. In this image, the spiral becomes the wire that connects the two pieces of wood. It represents the inner process which is gathering pace and engendering professionalism during training, and which emerges as that strength which draws on past life experience, having transformed it into classroom management, into creative teaching methods and insight into the nature of one's pupils as well as into those other qualities that are called upon in teaching.

In teaching, two worlds become connected: the spiritual, whence comes the inspiration needed to teach in a non-

---

★For further thoughts on the distinction between teacher training and teacher education, see pp. 63, 73f, 207.

prescriptive way, and life in the classroom (theory and praxis, to put it in more desiccated terms). The inner activity and skill constantly exerted by the teacher makes her work efficient. The 'pegs' of good teaching are put to the test when, later, the pupil-become-adult's inner powers of understanding, tenacity, integrity, commitment, environmental awareness, insight, discernment, good taste, fellow feeling, ethical stance, application, consideration, determination, are subject, as they bite on the clothes line of life, to the tempestuous onslaughts in modern society that blow from one direction or another. The theme in all these variations is *transformation*—the essence of what happens during teacher training to enable the student to identify, harness and develop her own inner powers in readiness for the task ahead.

This was the setting in which the climax of the graduation evening came when (all beautifully wrapped up in skitlike format) the mature student referred to above explained the 'esoteric' meaning of LWTTS: *Leaving Wholly Transformed This Saturday!* And how—like 'poor Yorick', the jester in *Hamlet*—the remark 'set the table on a roar'! Such a person is taking the 'bread of life' out into the world: the need for and the practice of inner work in the life of the teacher. However, we are all human. All-too-human on occasion. And while children can experience the teacher's inner striving, and without question blossom from it, we ourselves can get vital support from the building up of the community of teachers, both in each school through faculty meetings etc. and, when circumstances permit and are genuine, at teachers' conferences nationally and internationally.

It is indeed a moment to be alert to and thankful for when a colleague passes you the butter. For *teachers shall not teach by bread alone!*

7. Professional Meditative Practice

Teacher Training—Evaluation—Objectivity—Workdays—
Rückschau/Review of the Day—Self-knowledge—
Voice Control

'It was good backwards!'
People were filing into the main auditorium at the
Goetheanum, the High School for Spiritual Science near
Basle in Switzerland, the world centre for work arising from
Steiner's research. The centre was formed near the beginning
of the twentieth century. This particular occasion was the
morning after the day I'd given my maiden lecture at the
Goetheanum and the flood of feedback continued for several
days as I met colleagues new and old from across the world.
The above comment was made by the director of one of the
training courses for Waldorf teachers in the United States,
who entered the great hall looking fresh, jovial and bene-
volent from a good night's sleep as he came to thank me for
the lecture. It caused two immediate vistas to open up. One
of these was personal, the other a veil-lifting vista of the
teacher's inner life.

One of the unanswered questions which keeps dogging
me whenever I meet fellow teacher trainers in any formal
sense is: What advice might Steiner have given regarding the
esoteric life, not of the teacher—of which there is a wealth in
the public lectures as well as much given on other occasions—but of the teacher *trainer*? I refer to initial training, that
which leads to a qualification in Waldorf education at the
outset of the teacher's career (*Ausbildung*). For me, albeit a
non-German scholar, the *aus* of the German expression for

initial training has all the connotations of preparing to set off on a journey—in this case often a life journey with its necessity for both inner and outer preparation. This is in contrast with the *Fort of Fortbildung* (teacher education), which has the connotation of continuation, of going ever further in the saddle of professionalism, again in an exoteric as well as in an esoteric sense. Though the two (exoteric and esoteric) strongly dovetail, the latter necessitates inner work that the teacher undertakes as she carves out periods of quietness, in the bustle of a notionally '9–5' profession that can begin actually well before sunrise and continue until long after sunset. The former (exoteric) is cultivated in company with colleagues at regular weekly meetings, half-termly *workdays* (as INSET days were often called before the obsession for acronyms crept into the language, often smothering the layman with a blanket of unknowing), and nationally organized refresher courses and conferences, etc.

Several years ago, the work of Waldorf teacher training in Britain became amalgamated at national-meeting level with that of teacher educators (i.e. peripatetic advisors— even the nuts and bolts coordinator of the advisory service attended). This seemed a recipe for crowding out the inner work of the two professions, as more and more of the consequences of the evaluation malaise that was stifling creativity in so many areas of life came onto the agenda. Not that the teacher's inner life was ignored, but that the time devoted to it was limited, often severely, and the manner of discussing it—despite it being of innate value, with inspiring contributions from one or two colleagues— bore such a strong resemblance to the way it is discussed in weekly meetings of Waldorf faculties that how the element might be tackled in teacher training seemed to be virtually lost sight of.

★ ★ ★

The world conference at which the above casual yet con-
cretely valuable encounter took place was for teachers, and
was not concerned with initial training. My colleague's
remark ('good backwards') immediately gave one a profound
glimpse into his inner life. This is not necessarily a given in
human encounters, certainly not of the passing-in-the-
corridor sort. Whether one is extrovert or introvert, the
subtleties of one's inner life tend to belong to that part of
one's being that one holds in reserve. The 'space' between
yourself and the professional partner(s) with whom you are
talking needs to be right before that reserve can be opened
up, before the sensitivities of the inner life can be shared.
Mutual trust, empathy and recognition of integrity all play in,
of course. Occasionally the veil is lifted from one professional
quarter or another, to reveal the importance of enhanced self-
knowledge for the teacher. In August 2006, for example, the
Professional Association of Teachers, at their annual conference in Oxford, encouraged teachers to take lessons in
voice control to combat children being put off lessons by
teachers who speak in a boring monotone. But such
examples are all too rare.

At that particular world conference, the leader of the
Pedagogical Section of the High School for Spiritual Science
addressed the vast gathering several times. He was Jurgen
Smit, a Norwegian, whose outer and inner stature seemed so
much more than that of someone from northern Europe that
it is easier to think of him as a boldly adventurous Norseman
ploughing the waves of the spirit than someone who merely
held a Norwegian passport. When he spoke, either publicly
or in private, it was as if a veil was lifted to an inner world, a
rare capacity and one much appreciated by today's generation

who are often entwined in trivia in their leisure and bom-
barded by bureaucracy in their professional lives. But to refer
to the workings and procedures of the inner esoteric life as
light-heartedly as he did, with a touch of humour that has
behind it the profundity of esotericism, is equally rare.

And that was clearly the case not only with Smit. I
realized that my colleague—and I will come presently to
where our long connection originated—had taken my lecture into his review of the day, not merely by looking back
over events in a mood of memory jogging but as part of
his esoteric discipline. It was moving. Steiner (not alone in
this) recommended that anyone wanting to make something of inner progress in life would do well to make a
practice of reviewing the day's events *in reverse order*.
Whether he intended this as a weighing up with a strand of
assessment weaving through the review or a committed act
of seeing things as they were as objectively, as impartially as
possible (to *re*-view), we can leave on one side. The German word is *Rückschau*. *Rück* refers to going back (you
'love to go a-wandering' with your 'rucksack on your
back'!). *Schau* is a word implying a certain intensity of
looking. 'Beholding', if somewhat archaic in feeling, might
be closer to the activity implied than just looking.
Window-shopping would be at the other end of the scale.
A vapid gaze. Glazed eyes, come to mind.

It is the younger generation in J.B. Priestley's *An Inspector
Calls* (a play which reached the peak of popularity in Germany when it came out!) who, through introspective, persistent questioning of who the *first* inspector could have been,
divest themselves of self-deception. The scales removed from
their eyes, they move on to conscience-awakening self-
examination, something the older generation are loath to
face up to. The play ends when clearly—with the second

inspector-for-real on his way—they, too, will arrive at unadorned, probably very discomforting, objectivity.

The teacher's *Rückschau* is of course connected with self— what he or she has witnessed during the day, but its purpose is to get beyond the semblance, to divest one's beholding of any aspect of self that gets in the way of objective reality. And to follow Steiner's advice, and carry the exercise through in reverse order, is a vital step towards the gaining of a higher (spiritual) perspective. One will often teach 'in the light of' the higher perspective gradually being acquired through the *Rückschau*.

★ ★ ★

And the personal vista? The jovially complementary greeting on that 'morning after' rather confirmed a legend that had done the rounds. When Werner Glas, the colleague in question, had been an Upper School student himself at Wynstones (a Rudolf Steiner School in Gloucestershire), an eminent anthroposophist had been visiting and poked his head for a few minutes into the school hall where a carnival procession was taking place. Spotting this, and himself part of the carnival, Werner, already testing in his teens the anthroposophical waters, collared the said visitor the next day and asked what he remembered of the fancy dress carnival costumes worn by the students. The visitor apparently saw the sincerity behind the adolescent effrontery and obliged with an impressive itemization of the parade of costumes he had observed!

I was totally unaware of this incident when I attended my first Steiner educational conference in 1958, a conference that was to be the turning of the tide in my own career from working with special needs to becoming some years later a Waldorf teacher. One of the occupants in the dormitory in which I was billeted at the conference obviously had an exceptional pair of lungs, so that even on the first night I had to arise and make my way through the unfamiliar darkness downstairs to the first aid cupboard and help myself to a wad of cotton wool—long before I recall there being ear-plugs on the market. That 'occupant' endowed with a special breathing capacity was none other than my 'good-backwards' colleague!

8. Taking Another Lick at the Maths Lollipop

Subtraction—The Four Temperaments—Interest and Learning in Waldorf Pedagogy—The Rhythmic Part of the Lesson—Child-friendly Names for Mathematical Signs—A Broad Curriculum—The Teacher's Research

'It's the only thing in Waldorf that I've come across that I'm not sure about.'

Experience shows that it is possible to pre-empt maths phobia through considering processes, rules, operations, signs, nomenclature and temperaments *à la* Waldorf. A new look at subtraction is pursued here as an example of this.

When Rudolf Steiner met with the teachers designate of the first Waldorf school in August 1919, one session each day was given over to discussions, principally about pedagogy. The so-called curriculum lectures had not yet taken place—a fact so easy for us fourth generation of teachers to forget when we have orbited the full moon of 'the curriculum' so dominantly that it frequently eclipses the sun of true Waldorf pedagogy. At the same time it was very clear that certain subjects were going to form part of the curriculum—a good deal of discussion was devoted to plant and animal studies in Classes 4 and 5, for instance. Moreover, it was self-evident that core subjects would be as essential in Waldorf as in orthodox approaches to education. Maths falls into this category.

This did not prevent Steiner, however, being as innovative here as elsewhere. In the said discussions he drew attention to the connection between the four processes (or operations) and the four temperaments. Apart from the sheer fascination of such a link, what are the pedagogical implications likely to be? It would be absurd to think that Steiner envisaged the phlegmatics becoming specialists in addition but leaving subtraction to the melancholics, or the sanguines hogging the stage whenever multiplication came along; or leaving division to those children in the class endowed with choler! For purposes of practical life we all need to be proficient in all four processes.

For a satisfactory answer it is valuable to turn to what Steiner elaborated on regarding the way the teacher rouses and maintains *interest* in the subject she is teaching. Without the children freely responding with interest, you may well be teaching according to your well-devised plan but learning may not be taking place in corresponding measure.

Temperamentally each child will respond to different situations. *Routine* is likely to attract phlegma much more than it will choler. *Challenge* on the other hand would be likely to bring volunteering cholerics to the front of the queue. *Variety* will fling the sanguines into their element immediately, but will probably leave the melancholics far behind. But *apprehension* may place the boot on the other foot—the sanguines mildly dismissive but the melancholics feeling thoroughly exonerated that they had insisted on a watchman stationed on the walls at all times. And so on.

However, viewed as a pedagogical 'tool', interest of a temperamental kind is not completely isolated, not confined to the interested party; it has something of a contagious effect on the other three temperaments. Imagine the four temperaments like four different kinds of iron filings. The teacher raises a topic which acts like a magnet, say, to the sanguines. They leap forward immediately towards the magnet, but at the same time the other three types cannot help themselves also being somewhat drawn into the magnetic field of interest, in their case influenced as much by the interest of the sanguines as by the teacher's choice and skilled presentation of the topic. The same principle applies in the case of each of the four temperaments.

This principle is undoubtedly amongst the most nourishing 'daily bread' of all Waldorf pedagogy. Without it, it is questionable whether the astonishingly broad range of humanities and sciences taught to *all* pupils throughout their Waldorf school career, both in main-lesson and in other forms, would be achievable.

★   ★   ★

From one quarter of the globe or another, maths teaching (and the standard of maths nation-wide) is frequently buffeted by the winds of criticism. This happened in a completely new guise when firstly the leading universities questioned the parity of esteem between A levels and the work-related courses that were offered in lieu of A levels in the 2006–7 academic year, and secondly when the Engineering Professors' Council objected to the cut in maths hours in the new courses. A cursory glance at the Waldorf curriculum will show that maths is a strong strand right from school entry to school leaving (even when this is at 18-years-old), and that is for *all* pupils. However, Steiner urged the teacher to find accessible ways of introducing each topic as it came along. For him, an enjoyable and imaginative approach to teaching/learning was a basic principle from the outset. But according to a recent report in the *Times Educational Supplement* (June 2007), schools were taking four years to respond to the Government's paper *Excellence and Enjoyment*, which focused on the need to make the Primary curriculum 'more fun and imaginative'.

With all these principles in mind, it was one day in November 2003 that I was contemplating the four processes for the umpteenth time in my life, prior to a session I was scheduled to teach on the London Waldorf Teacher Training Seminar (actually on classroom movement, as an ingredient in the so-called rhythmic part of the main-lesson). Though we tend to take the terms of the four *processes*, the four *operations*, and the four *rules* as synonymous—lump them all into the same bag and allow fashionability to shake them up from time to time—from a Waldorf perspective it is worth re-examining them.

The *process* is what the teacher hopes to make the child familiar with and adept at as an inner faculty. The famous 'beans' that Steiner recommended that the children 'play' with as part of the process of getting to enjoy number are, in fact, little *operations* which, being experiential and thereby engaging the will, awaken the children mentally towards becoming clear about the mathematical processes involved. The four *rules* are more connected with the format we learn to set out on paper by way of recording the operation, so that (a) the process is made visible, and (b) numbers that are in excess of what we can cope with mentally (either as regards their size or complexity) can still be worked out efficiently and accurately.

For processes, we need to understand the *concepts* of addition, subtraction, multiplication and division. When operating our beans we will start with something like, 'Let's count how many beans there will be all together if we make four piles with seven beans in each pile,' and then gradually have recourse to the kind of technical *terminology* we associate with mathematics—e.g. seven times four; multiply seven by four; seven lots of four; work out the product of seven and four. For rules we need *symbols* (initially Arabic numerals and the five signs $+ \; - \; \times \; \div \; =$). Within these three stages (operation, process, rule) is to be found a principle similar to the one pursued in the Waldorf method of teaching literacy: first the active (running, walking, drawing, enlivening the letter shapes), and then the less active (reading). In the case of numeracy there may be some justification for process and operation jostling for first place. At all events, all three aspects are clearly interlinked. Nevertheless, the teacher will do well if she is aware of where she is placing her emphasis at any given part of the lesson.

Against this background I directed my thoughts to *sub-traction*, focusing particularly on the last aspect: the rule. Even within a single mathematical culture (an odd concept)—the way things are taught in Scotland, say, as opposed to Croatia or Tanzania—one comes across two or three different methods that people have learnt to do subtraction. Take, for instance, the following (and here we are assuming for the purpose of this study and for simplicity's sake that the 'sum' cannot be done mentally).

$$
\begin{array}{r}
TU \\
54 \\
-\underline{38} \\
\hline
\end{array}
$$

The stages in following the rule of how to work the 'sum' out can briefly be summarized as follows:

Option 1
(i)   Starting with the units: 4 minus 8.
(ii) You can't.
(iii) Borrow (from the top number of the column on the left).
(iv) Cross out the 5 in the tens column and replace it with a small 4.

(v)   Write a small 1 in front of the unit figure making it 14.
(vi)   Continue in the units column: 14 minus 8 = 6.
(vii) Write this 6 in the units column answer.
(viii) Proceed to the tens column where the 5 has now become 4.
(ix)   4 minus 3 = 1.
(x)   Write this 1 in the tens column answer.
(xi)   Thus the full answer reads as 16.

Option 2
(i)   Starting with the units: 4 minus 8.
(ii)   You can't.
(iii) Borrow from the column on the left, leaving it vague if necessary as to how its borrowing comes about.
(iv)   Write what has been borrowed as a small 1 in front of the unit figure 4 making it 14.
(v)   Give back the borrowed 1 to the column on the left by crossing out the 3 and writing 4 beside it.
(vi)   Continue in the units column: 14 minus 8 = 6.
(vii) Write this 6 in the units column answer.
(viii) Proceed to the tens column where the 3 is now 4.
(ix)   5 minus 4 = 1.
(x)   Write this 1 in the tens column answer.
(xi)   Thus the full answer reads as 16.

Bearing in mind Steiner's view of subtraction as having an affinity with melancholia, when I was class teaching in the 60s, 70s and 80s, I taught Option 1 but used a somewhat different concept—which would arguably form a third option. I need not write the stages of this third option out in full for it is identical with Option 1 except that instead of (iii) being 'borrow' it becomes 'Give the 4 a ten'. Thus the tens *give* the units the ten they need. ('Poor old units,' thought the melancholic, 'they'll never manage unless I give them one of my tens'!) If something is freely given, there is no obligation to repay/return. Thus with Option 3, at a single stroke, Option 1 achieves something of an ethical flavour, and the very complex and totally obscure procedure of Option 2 is completely fly-overed—i.e. if the 3 in Option 2, stage (v) *had* lent the 1 of stage (iv) it would surely have been reduced to two(!) and where would that have taken us?

As demonstrated, the *rule* in the early stages of recording this kind of subtraction sum having only tens and units—the giving, borrowing, giving back—entails physically crossing out the tens digit which is giving/lending and adding a small ten to the unit digit which is receiving/borrowing. I believe that because of the thought forms that this rule represents subtraction is often experienced by children as the most involved of the four rules—even mystifying, certainly an anomaly. This can be as many as a third of the class on occasion. For them, especially, as much clarity and as little complexity as possible is desirable, whether at the process stage, the operational stage or the stage of recording according to rule. Particularly is this so in the early stages of maths teaching-learning where a launching pad is being constructed for mathematical exploration of a higher order later on.

So back to November 2003. In taking the three 'givens' of subtraction into consideration, I came up with what seemed to me to be a more Waldorf-like option. Thus the three givens are:

(i) subtraction has an *affinity with melancholia*;
(ii) the minus sign is written *from left to right*;
(iii) the left-hand column of a subtraction sum *always* works out (except if you're drifting into overdraft, something

that a teacher earning a handsome Waldorf salary would never be likely to do!).

The fourth option is therefore as follows.

Option 4
(i)   Starting with the *left-hand* column (in this case, the tens): 5 minus 3 = 2.
(ii)   BUT before writing this 2 in the answer column *consider.* Will some of it be needed in the next column?
(iii) In this case it *will* be needed, so *write only 1 in the answer and put the other 1 as a small number beside the 4 to make it 14.*
(iv)   Proceed to the units column: 14 minus 8 = 6.
(v)   Write this 6 in the answer.
(vi)   Thus the full answer reads 16.

In the final sum there are no crossings out. Though (ii) and (iii) in this option at first sight look complicated, they are fully in keeping with the melancholic's psyche. In (ii), before any figure is written in the answer the *result* of the subtraction has to be remembered—and as melancholics are noted for clinging to the past, remembering a single digit number for a couple of seconds shouldn't create a problem. In (iii) the melancholic's empathy with the needy unit (4) is evoked while the resultant remainder (what is put in the tens column answer) is also another aspect of the temperament's awareness (after something has been given away or lost, what is left?). Sanguinity is likely to give away and not notice the cost; melancholia will count the cost but will still give with an empathetic heart.

A few moments doing subtraction sums of various kinds on the back of an envelope should soon convince the sceptic that the method works for all examples, particularly something like 4003 minus 1262, a type of subtraction that can be something of a *bête noir* for some children if any of the other three options be followed. Thus we have a new rule for subtraction (Option 4) with, perhaps, a suitable name for the sign: *Mindful Mr Minus* who always looks ahead circumspectly—but also melancholically-empathetically!—before he takes the next step.★

★   ★   ★

The reader whose interest has been roused and maintained to accompany me thus far will surely be able to *add* to the four options for working out subtraction three rousing cheers for Waldorf? Well … not always! As an example of how a study of Waldorf principles can inspire new approaches to familiar territory, a few years after the above event I found myself presenting the fourth option to a group of teachers in the Canary Islands (who were attending a two-year part-time course on Waldorf education). The group of about 20 consisted mostly of local Spanish speakers but also a handful of German and Swiss ex-pats. One of the latter was uneasy. It's not necessarily pleasant to discover that a lifelong habit (borrowing a ten and not giving it back) is somewhat wanting ethically. Perhaps on this occasion I had stressed this side of the problem too forcefully …

Be that as it may, the teacher's unease only surfaced later during a car journey: 'It's the only thing in Waldorf that I've come across that I'm not sure about,' was her comment. The remark helped me to keep my vanity in check and also to renew my confidence in the paramount significance in Waldorf teacher training of the virtue of *individuation*, rather

---

★ It can help children relate more confidently to the signs used in mathematics if they are given imaginative names initially.

than simple belief—sitting in a lecture, taking notes and microwaving them at the end of the module in essay form in order to tot up one's credits. But I was immensely relieved (I won't say exonerated) when, at the conclusion of the course, it was *she* who became the first graduate to move from mainstream to Waldorf, opening a Kindergarten in the capital of the island where the course had taken place. At the same time I cannot resist observing that you don't teach subtraction in a Waldorf Kindergarten!

9. A Milestone for the Ego

House Building—Rubicon—Dornach and the
Goetheanum—House and Home—Dwindling Family
Life—The Prodigal Son—An Age-related Curriculum

'I visited the Goetheanum.'
It was a colleague who had spent a summer holiday in
Switzerland and had taken the opportunity to visit the world
centre for spiritual science (or anthroposophy), the terms by
which Rudolf Steiner referred to the world view to which he
subscribed and for which he did so much throughout the
whole of his life to elucidate. Already during the First World
War an international team of both employed and voluntary
workers put aside the differences of opinion, which had
driven the governments of the respective countries from
which they came into fatal conflict, in order to help establish
the centre.

The site was a short tram journey out of Basle and, at that
time, the main outer project was the construction of the
building which Steiner had named the *Goetheanum*. This was
to be the organization's administrative and cultural centre—
possibly a more exact way of translating *Hochschule* than High
School which has other connotations in the English language. It would house study courses, classes, conferences,
artistic disciplines, performances and exhibitions, lectures,
workshops, research and suchlike, together with the
administration services that would be required to organize
and accommodate such activities, and the everyday needs of
large numbers of people (around a thousand for main conferences and performances) who converged on the

Goetheanum. The architectural result is an outstanding building in every sense of the word, a building of a world order, which has attracted wide acclaim in the architectural world. There were two outstanding buildings to be precise; the first Goetheanum had been destroyed by fire and replaced, in a completely different style, in the late 1920s.

It was not unusual for colleagues to visit the Goetheanum—particularly on the occasion of educational conferences where teachers from right across the Waldorf spectrum came together from all over the world to renew their impulse, deepen their understanding of how Waldorf pedagogy answers the needs of the modern child, and seek creatively new ways of applying the principles of Waldorf as elaborated by Steiner as a result of his unprecedented insight into the nature of the child and his personally having put such principles to the test in his own teaching experience. When the Waldorf school opened in Stuttgart Steiner was advanced in years. It could both look back on and draw from the formidable contribution he had already made to education. Even at university—and Steiner had already done much tutoring by this time—one of his professors, Karl Julius Schröer, had given profound thought to education (extant in his essays) which appealed to Steiner, even though at first sight this connection seemed incidental to his more official studies which were all in the realm of science.

★   ★   ★

The conversation with my colleague had something unique about it, however, in that the remark about having visited the Goetheanum popped out in a rather incidental fashion when he and I were discussing his forthcoming Class 3 main-lesson, *building*. The modest projects often built by Classes 3 as part of their practical experience of building (a little play-house for the Kindergarten children, perhaps, or a barbecue hearth, or the laying of a course of bricks in a 'real' building), however vitally important from an educational point of view, cut a strangely small image in my mind beside that of the Goetheanum—toadstools at the foot of a sequoia, or a chicken coop beside some kind of towering Valhalla in sculptural concrete. Judging by the number of Waldorf pupils who become architects or builders, however, the handling of that one laid brick (if that's the only opportunity the teacher has at her disposal)—sloshing a trowel of cement onto the course of bricks below, checking the vertical and horizontal as the new brick is tapped into place, and then experiencing the mortar dry as hard as iron even before the next day, etc.— becomes a life-enhancing lesson for the 8/9-year-old.

But whether we become architects, nurses, bankers or entertainers, we all go through that 8/9-year stage. Steiner referred to this as the *Rubicon*. The ego of the child, the highest member in terms of spirituality, has hitherto been hovering, as it were, in its connection with the other members: the body, its life and its soul. Hovering does not mean not rooted. Even at the stage of the so-called 'terrible twos', one feels the rootedness of the ego in the *joie de vivre*, the persistent questioning, the bold sense of adventure, the frequent stubbornness, and all the other traits that we associate with the age. But the 2/3-year-old's behaviour is as if directed from without. As a symbol, the image of a marionette comes to mind where the ego is the hand that manipulates the marionette strings, all out of an ego-consciousness that is far removed from the pin-pointed awakeness of later years. This is why an exasperated parent at this stage in the child's development can occasionally feel he is battling with superpowers!

When it comes to the time of the Rubicon, the ego dives

into a deeper connection with the other three members. Though it might be pressing the image too far, the shift from marionette to glove puppet could be a helpful way of understanding the incarnation process. The ego—the *hand* part of the puppeteer's art—moves from outside to inside. Inside the physical body, the ego has, as it were, moved into its earthly home. There have been 7+ years of 'building' this home, this habitation, and the ego now becomes the inhabitant. The increased reliance on the child's own ego may have an added dimension of importance in those circumstances today where, sadly, homes are fatherless, families seldom share mealtimes, the intrusiveness of television prohibits family conversation, 'real food' has given way to the (microwaved) snack, and children 'get in the way' of work.

Dr Rita Gardner CBE, Director of the Royal Geographic Society (2007), in regretting the decreasing popularity of geography in the Maintained Sector, recently cited the big issues 'facing us all—from climate change to migration, and from globalization to Third World development' as the reason for her plea to educationists to reinstate geography teaching. This makes eminently good sense, though the reasons are external. From a Waldorf standpoint, Steiner claims that the experience of geography—which arguably starts with an awareness of one's own home and then spreads out eventually to encompass the globe—has *inner* (as well as external) significance, in that it helps the ego to become firmly incarnated in its three sheaths.* How overwhelming it would be for a weakly incarnated ego to be presented with the big issues to which Gardner draws attention—not to mention the ego's gradually becoming aware that each

---

* These, it will be recalled, are the 'bodies' Steiner referred to as the physical, etheric and astral.

human being is co-responsible, in whatever measure, for the shouldering of the problems.

The age-relatedness of the Waldorf curriculum introduces house building at this point in the third class so that, through experiencing the bricks and mortar, the foundations and roof, the doors and windows, the fitted fridge and kitchen stove, the laundry facilities and all the rest of it, the ego can feel more 'at home'. Even though many families live in high-rise apartments, it can help the child at the Rubicon to be presented with an image of a detached house in its own garden or grounds. Even push the parallel a stage further back into the 'story' of building and give the home a fireplace and chimney, rather than under-floor heating etc. The chimney stack aloof above the roof yet set in extra solid masonry is a wonderful parable, albeit unspoken, of the ego's potential— fire in the centre, upright, stoic . . . Add an 'h' to heart and in one stroke you arrive at 'hearth'! The logs that burn there are taken from living nature, so if you cooked by fire the heat from the burning wood had a *transformative* power on the ingredients of the meal. Such fire needed putting out at night. A curfew was the covering of the fire (*couvre feu*), like the soul's and spirit's departure from the sleeping body after the long day's work.

★   ★   ★

Presented in this way, it may seem as if house building were the archetype for all main-lessons (and so-called subject lessons, too: woodwork, gardening, mathematics, foreign languages, movement, etc.). Yet in a conversation some years ago with an Israeli colleague I realized that this was not exactly the case. He had trained at the teacher training seminar (*Ausbilding*) connected with the School of Education at the Goetheanum and, looking for the origin of the building main-lesson in Class 3, could only find a mention of *gypsum* amongst Steiner's educational work. 'Show the children how gypsum is mined, as a raw material, and then how it is put to practical use (in plaster for the walls and ceilings)'—or words to that effect. It is a good example of how the seed of true and pedagogical relevance in Waldorf can be creatively germinated, nurtured and brought to blossom in the classroom. Of course, it is equally important to understand the symptomatic relevance of a particular subject in the curriculum. One could imagine deflecting from the real purpose of the building main-lesson, as outlined above, by emphasizing the development of building techniques from earlier times to the present; this is something that could well be of interest later in the child's school career, but if it is overdone there is the danger of detracting from the ego-at-the-Rubicon parallel, which is of such developmental value in the third class.

This is not to advocate that there is only one way. It may well be that a particular teacher can find the language that the ego needs to hear, via descriptions of *tepee* and *igloo*. While it is only natural and vibrantly central in the Waldorf approach for teachers to bring their own life experiences and inclinations to each subject, one also has to decide on their relevance for the age and, where necessary, be selective and curb the urge to gallop off on too much of a detour. Life experiences—overnighting in an ancient Scottish castle, or tasting a glass of camel's milk in a yurt in Kazakhstan, or partying on a houseboat moored in a Devonshire estuary, or a night spent in a rondavel near the South African Kruger Park, for instance—might afford colourful variety to a theme which is after all universal: the constructions in which humans dwell in social harmony together and from which they conduct their lives. In most cases the teacher will need to supplement both knowledge and experience, especially the latter. Knowledge is increasingly available as broadband gets faster and broader. It can, however, have the result of decreasing real experience while increasing virtual experience (because of the medium and/or of the way in which the knowledge is imparted) if it encourages the teacher to err in the direction of downloading and then merely offloading information. Facts need to be correct, it goes without saying, but in the conveying of those facts the child's feeling needs to be addressed and that is best achieved through the teacher first enlivening his own experience. This can include inwardly animating the facts, as it were. In the case of building, there will almost certainly be benefit to be derived from some form of practical involvement, of taking your feet for a walk. My colleague chose to 'visit the Goetheanum', the home of anthroposophy.

The pigsty in the parable of the prodigal son was not only far removed from the son's home (his father's, that is), it symbolizes how he had lost the plot. While incarnation ensures, from the Rubicon onwards, that we move away from our divine origin (the father's home), it is a necessary journey on our road to freedom. The circumstances the ego creates in life, however, can be such that something of that spiritual origin can find a front-door welcome, a plastered wall for shelter and a hearth at which the love of friendship can enjoy warmth and through which the zest for life can be fired. Every time it will resonate the dual citizenship of the ego: that of the world of spirit beyond bricks and mortar, and that of the welcoming earthly dwelling place.

10. The Psychology and Physiology of the Septennial Phases of Childhood

Class 8 Play and Leaving Party—Pupil Initiative—
Shakespeare for Adolescents—Rite of Passage—Primary and
Secondary Schooling—Eleven Plus

'I've fixed it!'
It was a telephone call late one night. The boy on the other
end of the phone was so excited that he barely remembered
to say who he was, and as I had never heard his voice over the
phone before I'm not sure so sure that I would have recognized it without the name tag. Even then, it took me a
moment at that late hour to twig what he was talking about.

He was speaking about a rope. No ordinary rope. It was to
be the centrepiece of the opening scene of our Class 8 graduation play. In that part of England we usually referred to
the occasion as 'class leaving', as at the end of Class 8, the class
teacher and children bid farewell to one another. The pupils
then continue into the Upper School, and the teacher begins
the next phase of teaching. As likely as not she will receive
the new Class 1 from the Kindergarten and conduct them
through their first eight years of formal schooling.

With today's frequent changes in life, for teachers as well as
children, it is not unusual for a class to have more than one
class teacher during their time in the Lower School, though
the ideal still holds good that the two seven-year thresholds
(at age 6/7 and 13/14) are best accompanied by the same
teacher, for continuity's sake, for stability and for other
reasons—the social conditions being right, of course. The

odyssey of the teenager through the Upper School is likely to be successful if the psychological barque in which they are voyaging has been well constructed in the Lower School and, where applicable, in the Kindergarten. In the case of the class in question, the buffets and squalls of adolescence were already felt at the top end of the Lower School. This frequently happens at this age, but it should not be a licence for adult carers at home or at school to throw the qualities, faculties, sensitivities, consciousness and vulnerabilities of childhood overboard, like so many corpses from a slave trader.

In the 50s and 60s, there was still something reserved about certain aspects of Waldorf education. A Class 8 end-of-year outing involving a plane journey had never even entered anyone's mind, as far as I am aware. By comparison, nowadays, it hardly seems much of a feat, except for those parents who can't afford it, though this problem is often circumnavigated through enterprising fund-raising. The Class 8 leaving party has changed less, though the play is often scheduled on a different day, thus spreading out the demands on all concerned. On the other hand, a play plus presentations placed all on the same day could be argued to make the occasion more of a puberty rite of passage (the kind of experience that could well contribute to supplanting the excesses of modern adolescence—binge drinking being one of the latest concerns of the British Medical Association). But I have organized leaving parties in different ways with different classes as there is no set model, and I do not wish to debate the pros and cons here.

★   ★   ★

On the occasion in question we were producing *The Tempest*, probably one of the most popular choices for such an occasion (together with *The Merchant of Venice* and *A Mid-summer Night's Dream*—all from 'the bard's' pen). It was my first Class 8 and also the first time I had produced a play with 14-year-olds. For me, this entailed two major rehearsal problems: first, how to put on a major production with adequate rehearsal time *without* encroaching on the time that the fairly hefty Class 8 curriculum demands; secondly, how to keep 30 or so adolescents fruitfully engaged *and comfortably disciplined* during rehearsals when, say, only two or three are actually acting on stage.

Scenes separately rehearsed during breaks as well as before and after school partly solved these problems, but there was still the educational necessity for all the pupils to get a sense of the whole, and therefore to be present regularly enough to experience the flow of the full play. The main way I embraced this problem was to have a large part of the class seated on stage playing musical instruments. This necessitated careful scoring of the music, of course, so that Ferdinand (for example) had time to make his exit gracefully, slip into his orchestral seat without sending the music stand flying, take up his trumpet and be ready to tootle at the precise moment. On the whole it worked, though there was always the pro-verbial room for improvement.

The visual success of this theatrical device depended on the orchestra being invisible, of course. This was achieved through building a fairly vast rocklike structure behind which the coming and going instrumentalists could be 'lost', and which served either as a general background to give a sense of the magic island or, more specifically, as Prospero's dwelling cave. Spotlighting helped to give the illusion of different parts of the island; for instance, where the royal party came ashore or where the triangular collision of the two comics, Stefano the drunken butler and Trinculo the court jester, with the 'monster' Caliban took place. But no spotlighting, however judicious, could lose such a commanding structure during the opening scene—when the play begins with everyone, except Prospero, Miranda and Caliban (the isle's inhabitants), aboard ship on the tempestuous seas. For this scene we closed a mid-stage curtain. This, however, didn't satisfy either director or those young teenagers whose limelight flashed only here at the opening of the play when the vessel is *dashed all to pieces*.

★   ★   ★

The human being during childhood, lays down the foundations for developing the full potential of this precious and prolonged stage of human development. But such foundations are not like those, say, of a building—a base of concrete upon which brick after brick can be laid up to the damp-course and beyond. Human foundations occur in rhythmical stages, the psychological rhythm of willing, feeling and thinking being superimposed on the physiological development of nerves-senses, respiratory-circulatory, limb-metabolic. These are primarily seven-year phases, but have subdivisions of $2\frac{1}{3}$ years within each broader rhythm. These rhythmical accents are not, of course, isolated; the systems *interpenetrate*. There is also a degree of *anticipation* and *echoing*. Thus, psychologically the phase from 7 to $9\frac{1}{3}$ years primarily expresses a feeling quality but with a secondary accent of willing (as always with the first third of a septennial period) as well as a tertiary accent also of willing due to the echoing on of the will-predominant first seven years.

By the end of Class 8 the psychological spectrum amongst the pupils is complex, it being a transitional time with some members of the class still lingering in the $12\frac{2}{3}$–14 phase while others have stepped into the 14–$16\frac{1}{3}$ phase, and this is without taking so-called *acceleration* or its opposite (*the slow developer*) into account. Nor does it take the *somatic* development into account and its repercussions in the child's psyche etc. However, it is enough to strongly demonstrate, if not prove, that the pupil on the cusp of 14 (i.e. in Class 8) is by no means at the same stage of development as an 11+ pupil. If the latter (in the customary concept of moving from primary to secondary schooling) is deemed to be the point at which pedagogy should change gear and proceed at a fully intellectual speed, many subtleties and character-building opportunities in the child's development will be lost.

This is the sort of thing that the Bow Group (a right-wing think tank) evidently had in mind recently when they published their report *Wasted Education*, in which they attributed the serious increase in school absence (AWOL) in the Maintained Sector to the 'relentless focus on the academic curriculum'. In some cases of pupils going AWOL, I would suggest (if one seeks a genuinely positive explanation) that the young person is seeking to complement his or her intellectual development in ways—whether 'desirable' or not and however inexcusable—not provided in school.

Apart from the maxim of addressing and bearing in mind all three soul forces, Waldorf education accommodates this situation in various ways. For example, *aesthetic studies* raise the pupil's artistic talents into the sphere of thought. A *craft* such as metalwork, especially with iron and copper, makes demands on all three soul faculties. Similarly with landscaping. From this point of view, a major stage production is ideal—though educationists should never overlook the linguistically and therefore cognitionally demanding facets of *Shakespeare*. These if well handled can become a lifelong blessing, but if not, they can block something in the adult which could otherwise have access to the world's utmost cultural treasures, the sort of treasures that are indispensable in what is in many respects an increasingly philistine age.

★   ★   ★

The complex psychological constitution of the teenager has considerable bearing on what is attractive in so-called *spare time*—a misnomer if ever there was one, when life is so short, but let us accept the cliché for what it is worth. With this in mind, and with the commercial tug on the adolescent's natural (or pseudo-natural) inclinations, many Waldorf schools—mainstream, too—organize *after-school activities* that are educationally valuable alternatives to merely pounding surplus energy into a rugby pitch, which was one of the public school's solutions to the potential problem in the earlier part of the last century. Rock climbing, potholing and sailing, amongst other activities, have proved popular and beneficial in this respect. Such activities, it goes without saying, have found good homes in other approaches to education.

One of the boys in the class in question belonged to the school's sailing club. Without putting two and two together, as it happened, I had cast him as one of the sailors in the shipwreck scene which opens the play. It was *his* voice that came enthusiastically over the phone that night. I could hardly wait to see what he meant by 'I've fixed it.' Had I not had a hundred-and-one loose ends to attend to, it being the eve of our class leaving party, I would have shot over to the school hall there and then to satisfy my curiosity. As it was, it had to wait till the next morning. I opened the stage curtains and saw the ropes he had rigged up; they were dangling down from the spars, I presumed. One of them terminated in a writhe of rope whose intricacy (to my layman's eyes) must have rivalled Alexander the Great's proverbial Gordion Knot.

The illusion of being on board, combined with the lightning flashes, the deck seemingly heaving and throwing crew and passengers hither and thither, and stage thunder crashing violently above our discordant effort at orchestral storm-simulation—excitable, poor intonation, I suspect, as well as the carefully composed discords!—was now complete. I hope Shakespeare would have been impressed. The audience and class teacher certainly were.

Tucked away in my memory, the whole incident reminds me of the pedagogue who remarked that it was in the teacher's gift to show adolescents the ropes, and then rejoice in seeing his charges clamber up them higher and more assuredly than he himself would ever be likely to succeed in so doing.

CHILDREN AND TEACHERS

11. 'Rights of the Child'

Adaptability—A South African Township—Early Years— Inspection—School Facilities

'We are standing in a queue.'
The sun was blazing—one of those crisp early Cape Town mornings with not a hint of sultriness. After my lecture at the Centre for Creative Education, at that time South Africa's only teacher training course, which had attracted a fine group of students from various ethnic backgrounds, I was invited to visit a Kindergarten in a nearby township. It was still early days in the Mandela regime and 'township' signified little more than it had in the past: row upon dishevelled row of extemporized shacks with minimal facilities for the crowds who thronged there. My white driver waved to the many familiar faces as we threaded our way through the narrow dust tracks. They were hardly discernible spaces for occasional vehicles—it would certainly be an insult to the pain and deprivation of the township folk if I called them lanes or streets.

It was not my first visit to a South African township. That had been way back in 1981 (to Soweto). But it didn't take much imagination to extend the culture shock of outer impressions towards the thought: What must life be like? Yet the warm welcome we were given at the Kindergarten entrance belied any idea that deprivation must preclude joy.

There are aspects of 'standing in a queue' that bear something of a resemblance to standing on an escalator packed with commuters. I don't need to go into all of these, for the similarity ends with the long row of faces. The

township Kindergarten queue was within sight of an encircling horizon of hovels, while the escalator commuters were
making use of part of a high-tech infrastructure. The black
township countenances shone with inner vigour (those not
only of the children but also of their adult carers), while many
of the white countenances—particularly those in the most
expensive capital in the world—betrayed inner hollowness of
some unfathomable kind. This goes repeatedly and poignantly deep. Like anyone who lives within commuting distance of London, I suppose I must have travelled on some
thousands of 'underground' escalators and therefore seen
some millions of people whose way of life is rooted in the
West. The general impression is one of a thriving well-
dressed population. But well-dressed has to embrace a predominantly dowdy colour impression—dozens of shades of
black over indigo jeans for most of the year, with little colour
to relieve the gloom—and, on top of this, glum, empty
expressions on their lonely faces. The massive amount of
sympathy called for in the two cases relates to different
members. As is suggested by the incident that follows, the
township dweller's suffering stems from the appalling outer
conditions of where he has but little option but to call his
home. By contrast, it is the lack-lustre soul life of the affluent
commuter that gives rise to concern, as he stands mute and
'static' on his escalator or by his conveyer belt or slumped
before his TV screen with eyes glued to a Cup Final replay.

When one thinks of the emphasis OFSTED inspectors
place on school facilities—measured in cubic metres, numbers of toilets, record cards and such like—one can't help
smiling at the township Kindergarten queue leading to the
one bowl of water, placed on the naked baked earth, as the
means of washing some dozens of busy hands for snack time.
Smiling? The contrast and the bitter reality can bring tears

welling to the eyes. One couldn't, of course, wish OFSTED to lessen its care of the hygienic, non-educational trappings that surround school life. But if the birth that Christians celebrate on the 25 December—*still* celebrate after more than 2000 years—could take place successfully beside a manger, one wonders when the new impulse that education is in dire need of will be born in its cradle unsmothered by materialism.

★　★　★

I've mentioned the dozens of busy, grubby hands, but not the corresponding dozens of stocky (despite a degree of malnutrition) little legs and feet, all so clearly exposed as I stood near the back of the queue, enjoying the scene. How to describe that line-up? Firstly, one had to admire those Kindergarten teachers, strategically placed, making a magnificent virtue out of the desperate lack of facilities (the orderliness, the cleanliness, and their *devotion* to cleanliness); and the calm, velvet-touch manner in which they disciplined. But it was pea-sized discipline beneath a pile of mattress-thick love for their protégés: discipline that 'harnessed the will'. Secondly, the children. They obviously felt secure in the straightness of the line. It was clear when their turn would come—and not a word of chivvying was necessary. Not that the line was as straight as a laser beam. It was more like a bowed cello string, bending and bobbing, throbbing and vibrating, as the lively enthusiasts for clean hands before snack time stood there, singing at the tops of their Xhosa voices.

It took my ears some time to tune in. When they had done so, I detected repetition. (Immediate, unadorned repetition is a good way to school the will.) On enquiring what the words of the vigorous jingle they were chorusing meant, I was told, with loving pride and admiration shining from the eyes of my informer: 'We are standing in a queue!' Standing, as I've indicated, was a complete misnomer if you applied it to the outer scene—the queue advancing slowly but surely, the tiny feet all but raising dust as the itch to dance tickled toes and heels, the curly heads bobbing to get a glimpse of whose turn it was to be at the water bowl now. But psychologically, the expression was spot on; the *queuing* stood there as an unassailable, unshakeably invisible formative principle, in which the life of a 5-year-old could expand to the fullest.

That is education. Let the politicians pile up their rules and regulations regarding the outer shell as they please—all notionally to do with the *rights of the child*. But let the *educational principles* be free of bureaucratic surveillance so that when the caring teacher brings the principle she is working with into creative birth each day anew, like a vibrating cello string, the children are free to experience the soul's melodic development—but within the limits (which, paradoxically, are not far from limitless!) of the cello's tuning peg at one end and the bridge standing proud above the sound holes at the other end. Lessons will then stand a good chance of being in tune with the age and will resonate with spiritual reality. It may seem an odd way of putting it, but surely every child can claim some birthright to 'join a queue' that leads to an education where the teachers understand, treasure and indefatigably nurture the profoundly human nature of those in their care—not only those privileged to be in a 'township' Waldorf Kindergarten.

12. 'Mood of the Fifth' and the Pentatonic Scale

The Young Child—The 'Nursery'—Adapting to Other
Cultures—Lullaby—The Aged Simeon at the Temple—
Government Funding

Be-emek . . .

The sun, with golden stride, was receding into the molten
wonder of evening, while nature swung her wafting censors
of white jasmine and frangipani. In the welcome breeze, the
women of the kibbutz strolled, pushing their lightly clad
babes in delicate contraptions whose design was as far from a
cosy European perambulator as you could imagine, while
from somewhere behind candle-glinted windows there
seeped the tones of a soft lullaby, invoking sleep. A giddier
mixture you couldn't have devised: the effusion of scent, the
release from the stifling hours that had imprisoned the day,
the soft shoulders of dusk, and a mother's evensong.

Those who flock from various parts of the world to a new
nation state (these mothers were the second generation, of
course), though tracing Jewish ancestry back to biblical
origins, do not necessarily bring all aspects of culture with
them. By definition, modern Israeli culture does not include
all the folk songs and children's nursery rhymes in its wake
that must have existed in the earlier times of the Jews. Back in
those pre-Gulf War days the younger generation, men and
women in their twenties, were creating a child-friendly
culture for their young families.

Certainly, the traditional songs for Passover, the Sabbath

meal on Friday evenings, Barmitzvah, and similar religious milestones of daily life, had been handed down. There was more singing in the family circle than you would find in an average home in England, a country exceedingly rich in folklore but whose cultural traditions in family or community have mostly fallen by the wayside, ignored both by the Scribe of the sophisticated intellect and the Pharisee of media and movie adoration.

Included in the founding of this particular kibbutz— *Harduf*, the Hebrew word for oleander—was a strong anthroposophical impulse. It nurtured—and still does— many practical activities arising from anthroposophy: bio-dynamic agriculture, a wholefood restaurant, therapeutical work with and residential homes for the disabled, a school of speech and drama, an anthroposophical medical centre, and so on. In the 80s the first Israelis to have found in anthro-posophy a practical way of life which they wished to cultivate in all its detail were coming over to Europe for initial training. They were mostly single but occasionally came with young families. It was the latter group who felt the urgent need to establish Waldorf education in the country, and with exemplary thoroughness and mammoth personal effort they did so, mostly training in Switzerland and in two or three training centres in the UK.

It was through such contacts that questions came my way as to how to adapt anthroposophy to Jewish-Israeli culture. Perhaps 'adapt' gives slightly the wrong flavour. Just as, ideally, the translator (certainly of literature) should be able to go to the roots of the writer's thought and from it produce a shoot in the new language as strong and characteristic as that in the original, so too those pioneers in anthroposophical activities in Israel sought the very foundations of anthro-posophy and at the same time those faculties within themselves that would bring anthroposophy to birth anew, so to say, from first principles. It is all too easy for us in Europe and the West to sleep through this vital procedure. We can find ourselves simply bearing the anthroposophical pine-logs in some rather wooden form (if we're honest about it) that we've been gathering from the forest floor of our pre-decessors, and following, in Good King Wenceslas-style, those footsteps which lead through the 'dinted snow' of works of reference, and the 'stronger blowing wind' of bureaucratic assessment. (And I am speaking of a time well before the present phase, where assessment culture has reached such a peak that some authorities in Britain, including the Qualifications Curriculum Authority (QCA), have gone to the extent of farming out the marking of some of the growing numbers of assessment papers as far afield as Australia, India and the USA!)

For the Israelis themselves, therefore, it was not a 'simple' matter of adapting what Steiner had given to the teachers in southern-central Germany way back in 1919 and the years that followed—a kind of computerized 'translation' of an anthroposophical approach to education. Particularly was this the case if they were going to get a frontier-fighting government to agree to give financial support to Waldorf education—which was their avowed intention (and which succeeded in a remarkable way). But rather they had to *reach the source* (and find ways of funding it) with what seeks to come to birth in the modern State of Israel—something like finding the princess's pea far beneath all the thick mattresses of the Jewish vote in Washington, Zionism, and the inter-minable territory squabbles, the fierce aggression likely to flare up at any moment on any one of their borders (Jordan excepted), and so on. They succeeded, not through appointing an extravagantly paid lobbyist whose insufficient knowledge of Waldorf might have resulted, unwittingly, in selling the soul of the education for 'thirty pieces of silver' but through *teachers negotiating with the Ministry*, occasionally enrolling the help of a Senior Academic Consultant whom they had appointed from overseas.

★   ★   ★

But to return to the intimate lullaby music of the kibbutz at eventide. For many ears, popular or well-known Jewish songs fall into two categories: the exquisitely introverted Hassidic-sounding genre; and the modern equivalent of King David the Psalmist, dancing to cymbal and shawm before the altar of the Lord—namely, the popular music which you can gulp down cheaply in hourly doses as you swelter in the bus going up from Haifa to Jerusalem. Both these genres are, of course, as far removed from what Steiner had in mind as appropriate for small children as a vineyard is from Antarctica. Not that such music was something glibly explained. He coined the term *mood of the fifth* to encapsulate the psychological/spiritual circumjacence of the small child. It's something 'out there'. If from a candlelit room it would be possible to remove both candle and candle flame, the light you'd have left would be where the mood of the fifth lives. With a young child nursed in your arms, there is something even less tangible than the cocoon of warmth that impresses the state of being of the child, something that Rembrandt captured when he painted the blind Simeon taking up the child Jesus into his arms at the entrance to the temple. 'Lord, now lettest thou thy servant depart in peace,' are the words that Luke the Evangelist quotes. The mood of the fifth is not the 'departing' part of Simeon's song, with its Victorian connotations of RIP, but the 'in peace-ness', long-awaited by an advanced soul—the blind *seeing* salvation.

In a lecture to teachers of music, Steiner pointed to the pentatonic scale as providing the wherewithal, potentially, for this mood. Yet it often remains illusive to contemporary western consciousness. Before you can pour milk into your tea—a noble English habit!—someone has had to milk the cow, it goes without saying. Similarly, the pentatonic scale is not yet the mood of the fifth. It needs 'milking', and will yield the right mood to the one whose knowledge of the young child is intimate, who has seen the 'salvation' of the future of humanity in the healthy development of the young child, who has realized the preciousness of those very first years and is willing (against all odds in the fast-moving pressurized pace of modern life) to invest *time* to nurture them.

Thus, *milking*. Fuse all that with the spirit of the Hebrew language and, given a little musical know-how, lullabies will flow into the churn of modern culture (other children's songs, too). That is what invoked sleep as part of that unforgettable kibbutz scene, softly winging on the dusk-blessed air. *Be-emek* ... A world première: the performer, a devoted mother; her aim, to endow the child (with the help of music) with the security of its heavenly home; the programme note, not read but divined by the child with closed eyelids; the unseen but all-seeing audience, an angelic host; and the sponsor, that most extraordinary of human mysteries—sleep.

13. Burning the Midnight Oil

Stages in Learning—Productive Homework—Marking
Books—2/3-Day Rhythm—Burdensome Paperwork—
Creating Personal 'Textbooks'

There was only one left.

The torrent of protest against testing has seldom reached the
intensity that culminated in June 2007. The General
Teaching Council (GTC) pointed out that tests placed an
'unnecessary burden' on pupils. The Royal Society, while
regretting the declining popularity of maths and science, took
a swipe at testing as 'stifling creativity'. Professor Sir Al
Aynsley-Green, the children's commissioner for England,
went as far as calling for the 'regime to be scrapped', the
'incessant pressure of exams and tests causing children to feel
under enormous stress'. The Institute of Physics submitted a
complaint to the Commons Education Committee that
pupils' motivation and enjoyment was 'damaged by the
frequency' of testing. The Institute of Educational Assessors,
which represents 3500 examiners, sharpened the blade of the
guillotine most of all—and incidentally came closest to
Waldorf praxis—telling the Committee that 'all external
exams' before the age of 19 should be 'phased out'. All this
was swelled, of course, by a vast chorus of less high-profile
voices. Being interviewed on the radio at the time, the
Schools Minister, representing the Government's view,
seemed about as sympathetic as a medieval torturer operating
the rack on which a Knight Templar was anguishing. One
wonders why. Is there a subsumed fear that the teaching
profession would not have the inner resourcefulness to fill the

vacuum that would result from scrapping the whole regime? This surely boils down to the need for teachers to develop imaginative *foresight* in their methodology or, as Warwick Mansell argued in his *Education by Numbers: The Tyranny of Testing* the need to encourage creative and inspirational teaching. Capping it all was the statement of Professor Alan Smithers, who had sat on the National Curriculum Council and supported league tables at the time of their introduction: with the benefit of 'hindsight' he had made a mistake; the less measurable aspects of schools had 'got marginalized'. In the interim, the mass educational graves...

Creative teaching and the box-ticking, bureaucracy of form-filling, record-keeping regulation-swamped, trust-bereft world spermed by the present nanny state are not the best of bedfellows. Yet both diametrical opposites have their place and need to be kept in balance through a centre-focused consciousness. A world-class cellist will have an agent to lighten the burden of administration entailed as a result of performing the Dvorak cello concerto in Sydney one day and the 'the Schumann' in Los Angeles a few days later. But what about the humble mathematician in inner-city Amsterdam teaching his quota of lessons, preparing them beforehand, marking homework afterwards, and more than likely having taken on the task of an examiner in the summer holidays to eke out a salary which may put butter on the bread, an olive or two in the salad, but leaves little margin for 'extras'? Fortunately not all paperwork in a teacher's daily routine is a loathsome chore—the slime left in the wake of forest-devouring, budget-swelling, time-annihilating, energy-sapping, spirit-maiming, bureaucratic dragons.

There is the so-called 'marking' of children's work, which gives the teacher glimpses into each pupil's soul qualities; she sees it in their very handwriting and the orderliness (or lack of it) with which the work is set out. She sees it in the books themselves, well-kept and clean or grubby, dog-eared affairs with perhaps a forlorn slice of cooked chicken-breast flattened between two pages (as, to my amazement and disgust, I once discovered on looking through a pile of exercise books in a class whose teacher I was officially *evaluating*!). And of course she sees it in the content itself.

★   ★   ★

In a Waldorf school, the pupils' written work is an integral part of a pedagogical process that is related to Steiner's insight into the psychology of the growing child. Apart from any reflection to which the written piece of work might give rise when marked and returned—and of course it need not only be writing, for artistic work of all kinds serves the same educational purpose—it is the end of a threefold sequence of events. The first of these is the presentation of material.

On the face of it—and from time to time criticism has been levelled at this part of the methodology—it looks as though Waldorf has not advanced beyond the days of 'chalk and talk': no (or next to no) visual aids, no DVDs, no walls smothered with material from the school's resource centre, etc., just the teacher's voice and listening children. What justifies such a method apparently lacking stimulation? Since I have more than once referred to the link between *interest* and learning,★ here I shall dwell on the kind of inner activity which the teacher's presentation conjures up in the child. For it is the teacher's aim to appeal to the image-making nature of the 7-year-old's 'thought'. Her verbal presentation is therefore couched in *descriptive* language. (This works particularly

---

★ See, for example pp. 80 et seg., 136, 147, 162 et seg., 214.

potently, of course, in certain subjects: geography environmental studies, mythology and other 'narrative', history, etc.)

There appears to be a growing awareness of the value of
the child's inner activity, unaided (if not dampened) by a
profusion of visual stimulants. In 2006, for instance, the Basic
Skills Agency report *Communication Friendly Spaces* strongly
deprecated the 'chaotic environments' of many schools.
Elizabeth Jarman, author of the report, was particularly
sweeping: 'When I go into schools, the clutter is unbeliev-
able. It's everywhere.' 'People fall into the trap of thinking
children need a lot of things to stimulate them all the time.'
The Waldorf Lower School main-lesson teacher, by comparison, uses her storytelling—adjusted to whatever age—to
invoke the child's inner image-making faculty, thereby
increasing each pupil's individuation of the lesson's content.

There may well be ancillary approaches, but whatever
pedagogical method the teacher uses—a conversational
prologue which draws on the children's own life experience,
or a reference to some story that has broken in the media, and
which has some bearing on the topic about to be taught, or a
simple verbal link of some kind to 'where we got to yes-
terday', or using the reflection on work recently handed in to
raise the level of interest and expectation—the aim will
usually be to present *new* material more effectively. If it is a
main-lesson, the sequence of old and new will be a daily one
(with interruptions at weekends); if it is a so-called subject
lesson, the rhythm will seldom be one of 24 hours but a
similar principle is at work.

Similar but not identical. The main-lesson teacher has the
distinct advantage of the daily rhythm, allowing the fact of
sleep to play a more significant part in the pedagogical process. On a particular day (let's call it Day 1), a new topic is
presented—in science perhaps a new experiment, in history

the next episode in the period being studied, in maths a further stage in the grasp of a new mathematical principle, in geography perhaps the economic aspect of a region whose physical features, soils and mineral wealth, communication systems and climate have previously been gone into, and so on. Before this happens, however, the previous day's material will have been recapitulated and elaborated in some way, i.e. for *that* topic it is Day 2. This is not merely a matter of checking knowledge retention as might take place in some educational systems that favour testing; it is a matter of affirming what has happened to the Day 1 material after it has passed through a night's sleep. This touches on memory, of course, and this in turn will be connected not merely with factual thought—Hannibal planned to take the Romans by surprise by attacking them from the north—but with *feeling-enhanced thought*. How on earth will the Romans react when they suddenly discover that Hannibal's army is approaching from the very opposite direction to the one expected? How was it possible for Hannibal to carry out such a bold plan? What kind of a character must he have had in order to get his troops to embark on such a marathon of a journey in the first place? What did his soldiers feel like when faced with having to cross the mighty Alps, and all *before* any combat for which they had been prepared could commence? And so on. With their feeling-enhanced understanding, the pupils are then told about the great trek with the famous elephants, up into high altitudes, with the ambushing of mountain tribes attacking their strung-out flanks, and the snow and ice making their advance hazardous and every step of their descent precarious.

There is still one more soul quality that needs bringing into play if the educational experience is going to nurture the 'whole child', as Waldorf purports to do. This is the *will*.

Already on Day 1, the will is needed in attentiveness. *Attention deficiency disorder*, one of our media-compounded, increasingly common educational problems, is complex in nature, but it certainly involves *will*. The adult knows from studying the necessity of pulling himself together if, through tiredness or whatever, his concentration on a particular text starts to wilt. 'To pull' oneself together is a matter of will, not thought. Even thinking is mingled with will when we *grasp* the meaning of what we are studying. Similarly on Day 2 with the recall, though it is not will per se that predominates. Stage 3 takes the process much more fully into the will. Willed thinking now becomes thought-driven will, as in a written account, or in modelling one of Hannibal's elephants, or putting one's imagination of the scene into a drawing or painting, and so on.

There are not only various possibilities for harnessing the will at Stage 3, there are several options for *when* it will be brought into play. During the recall one teacher might write certain key words on the board in readiness for an essay. In such a case, Stage 3 takes place on Day 2—this is often referred to as a *two-day rhythm*. Another teacher will involve a *three-day rhythm* in order, perhaps, to plumb for greater depths of will through dwelling on the subject over a second night's sleep. Another teacher, on Day 3, might extend the third stage (of will-activity) into the learning of a poem which takes a month or so to effect, or a play which may take anything up to six weeks to produce, or a project which extends through a two/three week holiday period.

Homework in a Waldorf school is probably best used to carry a subject further into the will. Herein lies a danger. The talkative teacher can leave insufficient time in the main-lesson for the will to be engaged. Each lesson needs to be balanced in addressing all three soul qualities. This does not mean, needless to say that, in a 45-minute lesson, a quarter of an hour is spent thinking, a quarter of an hour is spent feeling and a quarter of an hour spent willing—guaranteed to turn out the ideal lesson! A Mrs-Beatonizing of the classroom! The amounts of time vary according to the age and the activity—that is all the stuff of creative teaching. Homework is often the most successful, however, in the Lower School—though this is not to go into Steiner's views on the subject—if it is mostly confined to extending Stage 3. Typically, a slot of 20 minutes in the lesson enables the child to get most of an account written, or a free illustration drawn; and another 20 minutes at home is required to complete the job. Some subjects lend themselves to individual research at this level, such as interviewing an elderly neighbour to hear their experience of social conditions 60 years earlier; or, to take another example, tracing the plumbing through the house to discover how the water system works from the incoming mains through the central heating to the drains which connect with the sewage. A well-activated will is a homework well spent. Not all Lower School children can concentrate their thinking beyond the ambience of a teacher-penetrated classroom mood. But potentially all can busy themselves with an attractive or well-prepared task.

The teacher's response follows. Her so-called *marking* may or may not need to include marks of correction (spelling, punctuation, arithmetical or grammatical slips), but the *remarks* are of prime value for the child. They mount up to form a kind of dialogue over the years, a dialogue which nurtures the pupil's progress and, through having to formulate her remarks, maintains the sharpened edge of the teacher's insight into the child's nature and the corresponding tact which that nature calls for.

★ ★ ★

What with family commitments, meetings, telephones ringing and all the paraphernalia which are part of the non-teaching day (let us not moan here about record keeping), the marking of children's work is often relegated to the end of the day—not in any derogatory sense, but for practical purposes. Sometimes, burning the midnight oil. Planning which day to land yourself with a stack of essays for marking—pressed chicken-breast pop-ups or no!—is an important part of *classroom management*. Even though I personally adopted the practice of regarding essays as an opportunity for insight into the child's soul nature, it sometimes demanded a considerable act of will to start marking when the rest of the family were long since asleep. However, the midnight oil has its bonuses . . .

The incident I have in mind was in fact a Class 6 essay on Hannibal's crossing of the Alps. The pile of books remaining to be marked was getting smaller, but as my eyelids grew heavier I needed that little something which would take my flagging will to the finishing post. The next book was an answer to my prayer. The essay was written by a very 'together' phlegmatic child (this refers positively to her temperament, and has no *temperamental* connotations). Her togetherness produced page after page of weary warriors and beasts trudging up the mountain tracks whilst warding off savage tribal ambushes. As it was something like the thirteenth account I'd read and marked that evening, the picture of the historic scene in my mind's eye would have filled a canvas greater even than Turner's mammoth oil painting in the London National Gallery, which depicts the event with the elements' vast swirling in an unprecedented way. *Almost* equal, I reflected, to the picture that must have loomed larger than life in the child's own vivid 12-year-old mind's eye. Minor triumphs were dramatically punctuated with disasters, the latter mainly befalling the huge elephants, who slid or crashed to their deaths on the ice-treacherous mountain slopes. On the final page—and by this time I couldn't have been more agog—she concluded with Hannibal arriving down on the Italian side, mustering his forces, the essay building up to a remarkable climax as he took stock of his elephants. *He counted, and counted and counted and counted . . . and when he had finished counting he found that there was ONLY ONE LEFT.*

By this time, I was in a semi-agony of silent hysterics, not wishing to wake the family by bursting out laughing. Particularly when I read her final comment, made after an ostentatiously stabbed fullstop(!): *He got furious.* I can't remember what remark I put at the end of her phenomenal literary route march, but I still feel a sense of joyful gratitude to her, certainly for bringing creative life into the 'wee sma' 'ours' that night, but even more for her presence and being in the class. If Paradise began with Adam and Eve, we are going to need to start preparing some indomitable spirits for the 'end of time'.

14. Benefits and Hazards

Ego—Rounds and Canons—Choral Recitation—
Alliteration—Nurturing Social Feeling—
Concentration Exercises

'Would you like to hear us sing our latest round?'
Of course! I waited while the class were divided into four
parts, though somewhat surprised, I have to admit, that the
offer came from the Class 8 class teacher.

The incident occurred on an educational tour of Australia.
The school had made two requests, both original in my
experience. First, would I attend an assembly of the whole
school at which each class would recite some poetry in
English and, afterwards, would I share my thoughts and
observations at a faculty meeting on the 'standard' (as they
put it) of choral recitation and the literary quality of poems
chosen? Secondly, after the assembly, would I visit each class
and hear them sing and play instruments, and later at faculty
share similar reflections? Both of these were hobby horses of
mine, though how the school had guessed as much, I'm not
quite sure. Be that as it may, the requests certainly led the
hobby horse to the water where it was more than content to
drink long and deep.

Choral recitation and singing are the two activities in the
school day that are guaranteed to have bearing on the *social life*
of the children, singing perhaps even more than recitation,
since as well as the whole group having to 'perform' as one
the voices also have to be in tune; whereas in recitation the
normal speaking voice, albeit in artistic mode, is all that is
required. Not that this fact of social cohesion is necessarily

endlessly beneficial. As children develop, it is within the teacher's remit, in the present historic epoch, to ensure that an appropriate degree of *autonomy* is also cultivated. Too much recitation or singing at a stretch can lead to the *group spirit* temporarily superimposing itself too strongly upon the individual—even snatch the lesson out of the teacher's hands.

There are various ways of redressing the balance, amongst which, of course, is the absolute essential of ensuring that each pupil is able to recite the poem or sing the song in question without the support of the whole group. Steiner even encouraged solo singing in Class 1, though this is not synonymous with singing a solo. Even singing a song 'row by row' can be a valuable device which calls sufficiently on the autonomy of the individual and obviates the necessity of going round the class one by one. After all, singing solo might be too exposing for pupils in the throes of puberty. Besides, there are often other artistic ways of achieving the same end.

In singing, the art form which can first be introduced in order to call on the self-dependency of the incarnating individuality but *in harmony* with the other individuals present and involved is *the round*. (A canon is a more enhanced type of round.) Why is this so? A round or canon consists of a melody which two or more people sing together but not all at the same time. After the first voice, which can be a group of singers—mostly this is so in class—has begun the second voice enters. After how many notes and whether at the same pitch or not depends on the piece, which is composed in such a way that the 'staggered' voice entries fit together harmoniously. The French round, 'Frère Jacques' is one of the best known examples.

Thus if we consider the psychological situation for each individual, *while* he or she is singing a particular phrase a second voice (or there may be more, as in Thomas Tallis's famous eight-part 'Glory to Thee my God this night') is singing something else. If each singer is not to be put off, they will need to be able to call on a sufficient degree of *inner tenacity* to keep their part going with the correct melody. This tenacity is formed from the ego. It goes without saying that the music itself must be memorable and manageable enough in the first place. After that point has been achieved through practising the round, usually with all voices singing the tune together in unison, then the ego comes into play. The joy of round singing is hearing the harmonic effect of all the parts (or both the parts if there are only two) *at the same time* as being one of them. While it is the soul in which the musical experience is engaged, it is the ego that holds together the more active singing with the more passive hearing. A canon demands more of the ego than a round in that the second voice enters at a rhythmically less expected—or, in extreme cases, *unlikely*—place.

Such demands on the ego are strengthening where the ego is inwardly strong enough to manage, but not if the inner strength is unavailable. (Carrying an over-heavy load would have a similarly deleterious effect on the physical muscles). Hence the introduction to round-singing when the child is well into the Rubicon experience in the so-called 9th/10th year as a means of calling on, and thereby strengthening through challenging, so to speak, the incarnating ego. This is an example of the widely acclaimed Waldorf principle of age-relatedness, as seen in this case from the perspective of how the ego affirms its place within the three other members of the human constitution, the soul, the etheric and the physical.

The same nuance, of enhancing ego strength, can be arrived at through other educational means too. Poetic *alliteration* is a great favourite. In earlier times, the peoples who produced alliterative verse were Nordic. In southern Europe the individual found more fulfilment in the social setting. Warmer climes supported this. Alliteration in northern poetry, with clusters of repeated consonants clanging like hammer on anvil through each line, gave the autonomous ego, through speech, a stronger hold on life. Today we think of Scandinavia, for example, as being more socially advanced. Examples demonstrate how the Nordic mentality favours the individual; the Danish parental choice in education, which was a pronounced feature of education already quite early in the twentieth century; the remarkable independence of the Baltic States despite centuries of Swedish, Nazi and Soviet occupation and oppression; the liberation of the woman in the Norwegian political system, and so on. Thus, socially advanced here means society recognizing the *independent* needs of its citizens in one way or another.

Exercises that require *concentration* are also introduced at the age we are considering. A simple example would be when a class moves in a circle. While taking five steps we clap only once. While reducing the number of steps from five to four, we clap only on the first two steps. The falling number of steps and the rising number of claps are now equal: three of each. And so on till there is only one step but five claps. The concentration can be increased by dividing the class into two groups, concentric circles walking in opposite directions. The first group repeats the exercise while the second starts with five claps and one step. One can imagine, as the years move on, developing such a concentration exercise in various ways, the second group, perhaps following the sequence of 7 against 1, 6 against 2, etc. *in the same time span* as the group who are working with the number five.

Mass consciousness, of course, mitigates against the individual. The cultivation of and pandering to this often starts insidiously through the type of toys on the market. In his *The Real Toy Story* Eric Clark argues that whereas toys used to stimulate the child's imagination through 'inviting' the child to be active, now they 'stifle it: the action [through the push button type of toy] comes from the toy, not the child'. Peter Wilby, who became editor of *The New Statesman* in 1998, concurs with this view—toys are killing creative child's play—and sees them as becoming coveted as a 'badge of status'. Once the market has the child in its hold, of course, it is not a huge step to thrust 'sexualized clothing and electronic gadgets ... to [ever] younger age groups', with the individuality constantly being undermined. In contemporary society, it is undoubtedly educational time well spent if we find ways of counteracting such inveigling 'charms'.

★   ★   ★

It was such an advanced level of concentration (ego tenacity) that the Australian Class 8 teacher suddenly demanded of his class. The poetry assembly was over and my tour of the classes to hear their musical items was nearing its end. Ten minutes to go and it would be break. The teacher had clearly cultivated a love of music in his class over the years, which was heartening both to see and hear. They performed two or three of their prepared items for the visitor and did themselves credit. Then in a gush of enthusiasm the teacher glanced at his watch and, seeing there were still a few precious minutes left, chirped, 'Would you like to hear us sing our new round?'

I was delighted with the idea—it is almost as educationally unfortunate to give up round singing too soon after Class 4 as it is to make unwarranted demands on the ego by introducing rounds before it is truly ready. So I wondered what was coming next. Why the excitement in the class when he suggested it? Well, they sang the round through in unison and sounded confident. I was somewhat astonished at its length, pace and intricacy and was already imagining a little musical feast. But it didn't quite work out that way. When a round is either too difficult or is launched upon too prematurely, one of three things can happen. The 'weaker' part gets hijacked by the more confident voices. Or it can just dry up. Or, in their determination not to be defeated, the singers get louder, normally rather raucous too. With this class a new variant surfaced as the round drifted into the familiar ego-strained disaster!

As each voice entered, brought in and supported of course by the teacher, as is only proper, they started off in grand style. But it soon became apparent that the round really was *very* new to them, to such an extent that the ego had to contend with the complex manageability of the music, alongside the shallowness of the memory, as well as the normal 'challenge' of the other voices. All in all it was too much. But, to their credit, no one dried up or got hijacked. Raucous yes, and how! But suddenly, like rabbits scampering into the holes of their warren at the sound of a shotgun, each one in the class clamped both hands over their ears in a sudden rush of musical panic, mostly with elbows still on the desks and therefore heads down so that they couldn't see the conductor. The result was musically as cacophonous as anything you've ever heard (though only the teacher and I were 'treated' to it!), for the budding 14-year-old egos had taken the law into their own hands—literally!

When the racket and the hilarity had died down, good-humouredly we said good-bye, thankful for the joy and exhilaration with which music had connected us both in its harmonious mode *and otherwise*.

15. *Waldorf Non-negotiables*

Adaptation—Israel—Cultural Relationships—Modern
Languages—The Role of Authority

'Class Brien!'
It was early morning in the Middle East. The sun-filled air
was crisp and clear with grand views of Mount Carmel in the
far distance earmarked by its pencil-thin tower pinpointing
the whereabouts of Haifa University. I made my way over
the crown of the hill on which the kibbutz had been founded
to the Waldorf school. That already sounds too 'established':
a Waldorf school in conjunction with a kibbutz, the latter
organization known the world over for its pioneering of a
certain form of communal living within society, and the
former still in a somewhat embryonic stage—albeit an
embryo that has proved strong, healthy and resilient. It was
early days for both enterprises. The Waldorf school consisted
of two classes and a Kindergarten. It was one of several
enterprises the roots of which the kibbutz was putting down.
The others were: a biodynamic farm, a wholefood restaurant,
a foundation seminar in the study of spiritual science and a
bakery. And more have since sprung up.

Both class teachers had trained abroad, one in Switzerland
at the heart of the Waldorf movement. Perhaps it was
because of this, as well as his own personality, that he had
gained the inner confidence, together with his colleagues of
course, to introduce the education to a country that prided
itself on world-class academic excellence, and could point to
a host of geniuses in several fields whose family origins had
been Jewish. At the same time, though Judaism has long,

unbroken *religious* traditions, a country as new as the State of Israel, coupled with the sharp-minded acumen that is characteristic of its people's way of thinking, benefits enormously in daily life (which is not so tied by apron-strings to the 'vote in New York' as is its politics) from an uncluttered past. Hence, what seems eminently practical, providing you have reasonably good contacts 'at court', is likely to get a fair hearing and a good chance of being accepted. This has certainly proved to be the case with the Waldorf movement there, which has never seriously looked back.

But we are leaping ahead. At the time I am referring to, the school was in its early trial period as far as the government was concerned (having achieved the supportive status of being classed as an 'experimental school'). It was, however, still very austerely housed in the typical prefabs of kibbutzim that accommodate a small family, each class having an entire building to itself, i.e. with all interior walls removed, except those portioning off the toilet in one corner.

★ ★ ★

It is the *form* of an ocean wave that moves (somehow!) through the water, which is not, of course, to deny the vast intercontinental currents that circulate around the globe— the water itself on the move. The *variables* in the oceans give rise to coral in one place and penguins in another. So in Israel, it was a matter of discovering, researching, studying collegially and adapting to the social, cultural, political, geographical and economic variables but so that the archetypal form of the education would still be undistortedly and life-givingly Waldorf. As Steiner had to negotiate with the Stuttgart education authorities in 1919, so it was in Israel, with regular contact maintained with the Ministry in Jerusalem. In such circumstances the negotiators need to be alert

as to what in the ocean is penguin, coral, sardine or nauti-
lus—which might be determined culturally or politically, and
here one can be on dangerously *un*pedagogical ground—and
what is the non-negotiable 'life in the ocean wave' of
genuine, unadulterated Waldorf.

The variables, to say the least, are fascinating: Israel with its
strong flavour that results from its being Asiatic (albeit in full
confluence with the hot water systems, nuclear power
stations, chemically-driven horticulture, etc. of the West); its
preserving its hoary, age-old associations (linked to its
archaeological biblical sites) that make something like the
centuries-old British public school system sound like the beak
of a feeble Easter chick tentatively tapping at the inside of the
surrounding shell; its pursuing a distinctly unilateral course in
many of its national policies (the despair of those who see the
regime as 'getting away with blue murder'); its being destitute
(if that is not too strong an expression) of folk culture (as
distinct from religious-linked laws and customs); and its
tangibly in-it-together social culture, as well as the close links
that still enable the family to coagulate in a way that usually
surfaces in (*and only in*, for the most part) communities in
adversity, a facet of life that is the envy of many a totally
isolated 'family' unit in the West—all of which can understandably give rise to a questioning attitude when it comes to
applying the Waldorf curriculum. Examples would be: What
relevance does Norse mythology have for an Israeli Class 4?
How do Israeli Waldorf schools steer their course through
the Old Testament (as the West would call it) seeing that it is
required study in that country from Classes 2 to 12 (the
requirement coming essentially from the authoritative
influence that the rabbis exert), as compared with Steiner's
indication that the 'book' should be studied as 'world literature' in Class 3 and not as directly impinging on the

religious life? When Steiner cites 'saints stories' for Class 2 narrative, what are Israeli Waldorf teachers going to teach as compared with what tends to be the sole diet of Christian saints whose biographies are frequently narrated in most of the West? What will the Israeli perspective be on history and subjects such as the history of art, all of which form such a solid and crucial part of the child's school experience? And then there is the question of celebrating the festivals in the Waldorf schools in Israel. There, as elsewhere across the Waldorf world, they are seen and experienced as invaluable educational assets in the rhythmical, social and cultural life of the school year—all elements which nurture different aspects of the whole child. The cancelling of Christmas (or the Jewish equivalent) because it gets in the way of tests—the preparation for which takes up to 44 per cent of the teaching time in some English State Primaries, as reported in the *Times Educational Supplement* of 11 May 2007—would not remotely find its like over there.

It is therefore imperative that the Israeli teacher become clear about the archetypal elements in Waldorf education (the wave-form) so that the variables—back to halibut, sardines, seaweed and dolphins!—still ring true.

★ ★ ★

The above is the context that brings to mind the anecdote alluded to at the head of the chapter, connected with the words 'Class Brien'. Very sensibly, the school had decided that the three foreign languages to be taught should be Arabic, English and German, the rationale behind the decision broadly being Arabic to strengthen immediate national connections, English to strengthen world connections and German to strengthen European connections, these connections in Israel's precarious position taking precedence over one of the languages being a 'romance' language (French or Spanish, for instance) which would have made linguistic sense.

It was a memorable joy for me to sit in on an Arabic lesson. The school had acquired a good friend and colleague (a head teacher from a large neighbouring Arabic secondary school) who came to teach Arabic in the kibbutz on his free days— Fridays and Sundays, the Arabic population being mostly Islamic and Christian. It was his lessons that were pedagogically inspiring. Despite having (at that time) no Waldorf training of any sort, his love for the language, equally matched by his love for the children, was so contagious that the children made headway. Instinctively he used much repetition so that the children became enwrapped, so to speak, in an aura of Arabic sound and culture. I do not recall even a flicker of anything that one might call disciplinary action or indeed the need for it. It reminded one of the apocryphal story of the head teacher who, on being asked by the school inspector what policies she had put in place for dealing with behavioural problems, brazen-facedly turned on the little man in his pin-striped suit and with defiance in her headmistress's voice parried his thrust with, 'Inspector, we simply don't believe in them!' And as far as she was concerned, that was the end of the conversation.

The key to the Arabic teacher's teaching technique, I worked out, needed two twists before it opened the door to success. I think I have described *his* twist sufficiently: the magic sound of the language emanating from his whole being, so that all the children in his class danced willingly and merrily to his Pied Piper enticements. The other twist was effectuated by the class teacher who, alongside his deep enthusiasm for inaugurating Israeli variables, also knew his Waldorf onions and thereby had instilled a lovingly *author-*

itative teacher-pupil relationship. Reaching deep down into the nature of the children, the principle of authority readily and touchingly spilled over towards other people—a secure feeling in the children which resulted in their being unconsciously willing to give the adult, as it were, the benefit of the doubt that he or she was *worthy* of being followed as an authority. Beyond the Jew, the Arab, the Englishman is a human being.

And that's how it came across to me in that air-crisp Middle-Eastern sunrise of a morning. After the class teacher had greeted the class with 'Good morning dear children,' and they had reciprocated with, 'Good morning dear teacher,' (using his first name, I should point out), his glance signalled to me that I should also greet them. I decided on (in English, my Hebrew not even stretching to a 'good morning' on such a public platform!): 'Good morning Class 2.' The principle of authority kicked in so strongly at this point that they cottoned on to the formulation—assuming, presumably that 'Class 2' meant 'dear children'—and replied in a heart-filled, sunny chorus: *'Good morning Class Brien.'*

Needless to say, not *every* visit abroad makes one feel that one is in a class of one's own! At the same time, a challenge here and there to help overcome one's vanity is always a good thing!

16. Literacy: Mere Decoding or a Gateway to Literature?

Teacher's Ambitions—Steiner's Expectations—'Classics' and Culture—Linear Thinking—Children Under Pressure—Openness in Relationships

'Son of Ivanhoe!'

The debate about 'reading age' swings endlessly to and fro, not totally unlike the trench warfare in Belgium, following the Battle of the Marne, during World War I. The linear-thinking-type view is that if the aim is to turn out citizens who are literate then the sooner their literacy education is started the better. And as government policy remains obstinate in some states, Britain amongst others, no amount of research that strongly demonstrates the contrary appears to de-entrench the thinking. Meanwhile, Waldorf education continues its well-tried and well-rationalized approach consisting of a steady introduction first to writing in Class 1 (age 6/7) and more or less simultaneously with that—though emphatically not preceding it—reading. It is one of the non-negotiables of Waldorf praxis with valuable longer term implications for the individual than almost any other aspect of Waldorf pedagogy and the curriculum which it teaches.

At a recent forum, a government representative asked the panel about this very point and the Waldorf reply—actually from someone who taught in the State sector!—drew attention to the ground-floor phenomenon of children who have been *put under pressure* to read in the early years certainly being able to decode the words. (There are the exceptions, of course, and there are the many cases of those who literally go through years of trauma at the hand of this method.) She commented, however, that decoding was not the same as reading if, by reading, you mean following what was being 'read' with interest and with understanding. Such cases are legion. By contrast, though admittedly statistically not so numerous, there are plenty of Waldorf pupils who, through the steadier and multi-informed approach, read actually without being taught. The impetus of wanting to read and being ready to understand, together with the *worthiness of the reading material*, build up the crest of the wave of the technicalities involved until it breaks on the shore of *becoming literate*.

To put the case at its most extreme—though this is not intended to lead to a distorted generalization—the early reading approach courts the danger of getting little further than efficiency in literacy and, at its worst, fuels the one-time conspiracy theory—now backed up increasingly by research★—that dyslexia in any of the 1 in 10 cases in the UK is a *consequence* (not a cause) of struggling to read. Be that as it may, the steadier Waldorf approach, practised in Finland and elsewhere, while being literacy-efficient, strongly suggests that.

The image of the First World War trenches at the beginning of the chapter was perhaps not ideal, yet even with the Waldorf approach to literacy (writing first followed by reading) the battlefield being experienced today in the book trade between (to put it pictorially and succinctly) the library

---

★ See recent research carried out by Professor Julian Elliot, an educational psychologist at Durham University. The head of the charity Dyslexia Action reported that disability allowances at university cost the system £78.4m per annum, albeit covering some disabilities attributed to dyslexic conditions other than literacy.

shelf and the media resource centre cannot be avoided. The pros and cons of the internet are too familiar to need rehearsing here. Here it is a matter of applauding the character-building quality of reading good literature, a quality as educationally valuable now as it was in 1919 when the first Waldorf school began. What the adult does with the skill, once acquired, is his own business.

★   ★   ★

The class I have in mind as an example had had a first reader at age 7/8. There was an enormous hare-and-tortoise-like discrepancy at this early stage between the fluent readers and the slower ones. This problem can be addressed by the (traditionally common) reading group. Certainly of value. I also felt that a *class* activity could be relevant and we went right through the rest of the Lower School with some book or other always 'on the go'. The method which worked well was to allow each pupil to read for approximately the same *amount of time*—with the very fluent readers, here and there, getting a lion's share. This meant that the class had no more than two minutes or so to listen to the slowest reading-struggler, which prevented any accumulation of frustration for those who wanted to get on with the story, while at the same time pre-empting any serious embarrassment for the slow reader. Not only that, appreciation (initially, of course, from the teacher) for the tiny steps of improvement encouraged the latter to take it calmly and do his or her best without getting flustered.

In this way, apart from the books which the children chose themselves to read from the class library, over the years we covered a variety of literature that was age-appropriate both in style and subject matter. Without becoming ambitious, however, I was aware that Steiner had very high expectations, if that is a fair way of referring to his curriculum suggestions—the outstanding example being Dickens in the original Stuttgart Lower School *in English!* Consequently, I had my eye on Class 6 as the year in which one could embark on literature 'proper' as distinct from children's stories written in a good but easily digestible literary style. The school library abounded with these, and they were popular amongst the children, so I felt my role as class teacher was to build a bridge to the equivalent of Dickens in a German Lower School. Indeed, why search further?

Considering this, and feeling that the class had not yet reached the inwardness that comes about with the onset of puberty, I placed Dickens slightly at arm's length and veered towards Scott. With an earlier class I had settled for the adventures of *John Macnab* by one of Scott's compatriots and greatest admirers, John Buchan. There were twinges of apprehension that perhaps I might be trying my luck to go into the heavier literary grandeur of Scott, but I thought that the colourfulness and fast moving drama of something like *Redgauntlet* or *Ivanhoe* would fit the bill. With all that in mind, as well as the part played by Sir Walter Scott in my own teenage escapism, I settled on the latter. The period in which *Ivanhoe* is set, being roughly coincident with the history for the year (which ends with the Middle Ages) and the sheer variety of incident were both elements in the novel that I thought would do the trick. Not only did it seem to measure up to Steiner's expectations, but it also resonated with the chorus of lamentation, sung by public figures, that the State school curriculum was constantly dumbing down elements that had hitherto contributed to the spiritual strength of the nation's culture.

Well, it got away to a promising start. I set preliminary reading, having given the whole story a rousing introductory send off. As we read aloud in class, I interposed where there were tricky passages vocabulary-wise. I ensured that the characters stood out in strong relief. I bridged the slow-moving descriptive passages (obviously not all of them, which would have partly defeated the object of the exercise) by giving a précis in my own words, or even took a turn reading aloud as teacher to move things on. We savoured the purple passages. We did some creative writing ourselves alongside some of the adventures. And we cantered to the finishing post! Fairly handsomely, I felt on reflection.

It was only much later that I became aware that all that glisters is not gold, and that my enthusiasm had been a bit over the top. One of the girls who, ironically, went on to distinguish herself in publishing, gently but pointedly pulled my leg on a very public occasion when we had the opportunity, not just to review the past eight years but to reminisce. 'And now, at last,' she said, with a smile that betrayed satire beneath its warm-heartedness, 'we can look forward to the pleasure in the Upper School of meeting *The* Son *of Ivanhoe!*' Few of the parents could have appreciated the reference, but as far as the pupils in the class were concerned it brought the house down—and removed a scale from at least one of my pedagogical eyes! It also speaks volumes for the *openness*, which is part of a true Waldorf ethos, in the relationship between pupils, parents and teachers, an openness which can only support the educational process.

17. Waldorf, the Arts and Culture

Adolescence—Aesthetics—Metamorphosis—Music and
Musicality—School Environment and Architecture—
'Childhood on the Cheap'

'At last!'
While working in Scottish Waldorf schools in various
capacities, on one of my travels I met a string player (violin
and viola) who was keen to combine forces in some way.
This led to the formation of a small chamber music ensemble,
which included Waldorf pupils, and some years later to a
concert which he and I gave in Nuremberg to where he had
since moved and where his large family attended the local
Waldorf School.

In an age in which culture has been largely flooded by the
media, it sometimes feels as if musicians are threatened with
the same Sword of Damocles that is frequently poised over
the heads of academia ('publish or perish'). Standards of
performance soar but are increasingly in the recording studio
instead of, as in former times, on the doorstep. Connecting
children with *live* culture, therefore, can be a problem for
families. Without that first-hand connection, the danger is
that the child will grow up in a kind of human vacuum. The
human voice comes out of a disembodied radio. The music
comes out of a disembodied CD-player. The actors flit across
the screen of a disembodied TV set. The adult conversation,
interspersed with periods of varying lengths of silence,
engages with a disembodied telephone handset. And so on.
All these are appliances, needless to say, that the children will
sooner or later become accustomed to and in some cases

dependent upon for one reason or another. But as an introduction, often already in babyhood, to *social* cultural life...?

If one lives in a culturally thriving metropolis and can organize both time and money, this vacuum can easily be countered: going to live theatre, attending live concerts, participating in live debate—shame that we need to signal the rarity of such experiences by using the word 'live'! Shame also, lasting shame, that there are not more *governments that sponsor musical activities* at school level, as happens currently in Sweden, for example. Unless something like this comes about, it is difficult to see how the death of live music in children's lives will be prevented. The policy of 'childhood on the cheap' will certainly need to be swept right away, in this, as well as in other, respects. Before the days of discography, Oscar awards, videos and the internet, the opposite of 'live' was *dead*—Plácido Domingo's recorded voice booming out of some electrical appliance is not something we associate with death, yet 'corpses of sound' emanating from a once live human larynx in the same space as the listener, with or without the 'help' of amplification, become a hardly questioned feature of the lifeless desert of today's culture compared with that which existed, say, in Beethoven's Biedemeier Vienna or in Nelson Mandela's homeland.

It's all right for us adults. We have the mature ego to make the choice, live or otherwise, and at the same time, if the latter, to realize that we are experiencing only simulated reality. We have the mature ego to confront the human vacuum with consciousness, that is, appreciate through concentration the 'performance' or simply consign it to 'background noise'—which is essentially what it is, one might argue, if we don't *convert* the sound into music in our attentive souls. A child doesn't possess that discriminating ego to the same extent. The younger the child, the more is this the case. Many Waldorf schools, therefore, try to address this problem by organizing cultural events in which children participate and which they attend, either as the class as a whole in school time or out of school time with the family. Much more could be done in this respect both to stimulate culture and to help put the human being centrally back into it.

★   ★   ★

But whether schools take up such initiatives or not, within the Waldorf curriculum there is ample scope for the cultivation of an appreciation of the arts. This is not merely art for art's sake—though there would be nothing wrong with that in moderation. Aesthetics lessons in the Upper School, in particular, give time and space to the study of the visual arts (Class 9), literature (Class 10), music (Class 11) and architecture (Class 12). These are the bare bones, so to speak; there may well be much more besides. The thread which runs through such lessons, though it may often be more implicit than explicit, is one which connects how *human consciousness changes through the ages*. We can, of course, quantify change to a certain extent by measuring such things as the production and consumption of oil, or the advances in sanitation provided on housing estates, or as the increasingly 'efficient' destructive power of so-called conventional weapons... As far as brain hemispheres are concerned an appreciation of art in its various forms takes us into a qualitative rather than a quantitative realm. Steiner regarded the former as being of inestimable value to the balanced development of the adolescent—or more precisely, the Upper School pupil.

The awakening consciousness that is central to the development of the child in the third septennial period is directed, through aesthetics lessons, towards the highest cultural achievements of the human mind through all ages of time. Through participating in such considerations—and it goes without saying that in the visual arts much reliance has to be placed on reproductions (mainly through the use of slides)—the whole soul life of the adolescent is enriched. However, another pedagogical principle cannot here be overlooked: that of metamorphosis from Pre-School to Lower School to Upper School.

The artistic experiences in the Lower School are deep-seated—the child paints weekly, draws almost daily, models frequently, perhaps in blocks, sings and plays a musical instrument as part of daily school life, lives in, moves among and experiences the school's architectural forms, speaks poetry in chorus each morning as part of the so-called 'rhythmic' beginning to the main-lesson and so on. Through these experiences, taken in through the child's emotional intelligence, a foundation is laid for the soul's *appreciation* of what has resided within it through *participation*. The principle can be extended backwards to the first seven years, too, in which the child experiences the arts as an integral part of life. The adult can work on her speech, formulating it as artistic speech. The space in which the Kindergarten takes place can be organized as an artistic space—from the entrance hall with its shoe-boxes and coat-hooks to the seasonal nature corner, to the orderliness in the teachers' room cupboards, out of sight but still contributing to the atmosphere of the building. Beauty is not 'preached'; it simply pervades every nook and cranny. Thus, art at this level is experiential, impregnated with life, as it were. So we have the three interlinked stages: 0–7 as part and parcel of daily *life experience*, 7–14 through *participation*, 14+ with increasingly informed *appreciation and appraisal*. It is self-evident, of course, that the first stage must continue to resonate in the environment of the second and third stages, and likewise the second stage must still form part of the curriculum (even if reduced proportionately) in the Upper School. At the same time, Steiner's advice that the architecture in which the higher classes are housed should be more 'utilitarian' suggests that the soul's experience of the artistic undertakes a journey from the outer surroundings (0–7) into the ever-awakening inner life (14+).

★   ★   ★

But now to return to the concert in Nuremberg. Bearing in mind the communal need parents have to fill the cultural vacuum of modern life, it was natural to see many comparatively young children in the audience. On such an occasion, they are not sitting listening in any *appreciative* way. Hopefully they will enjoy the music played in a concert they attend, particularly if they can actually *see* the musicians—the bobbing elbow of the violinist, the squirrel-quick fingers of the pianist and so on. Even so, small doses are probably the best for Lower School children. In this situation, enjoyment of the music-making is what matters, especially if the silent message comes across: society is blessed and enhanced by music-*making*. School presents the other side of the coin. Through *participating* in music in their lessons day by day an *organ of musical perception* is built up. This, of course, must be at an appropriate pedagogical level—probably and preferably pentatonic music at the pre-Rubicon stage leading gradually to a more 'sophisticated' repertoire. With this organ they supplement, albeit simultaneously, what their ears hear with what their growing musicality perceives. This will lead in the older children (Class 8 onwards) to an aesthetic appreciation of style, perhaps both the style of the composition as well as the manner of performance.

However, the danger cannot be overlooked of over-compensation for the disembodied cultural desert through which the majority of people have to trudge as they try to keep up with the mortgage payments. The eagerness to compensate can, of course, result in taking children too early to a public concert—without question with the best of intentions! Or expecting them to sit the concert through to the end. This is what happened on the occasion cited at the beginning of the chapter. For various reasons a 6-year-old boy was brought to the concert and was unable to leave after the first item or two—which would probably have been enough. Thus, when the boy's parent said, after the last item had been applauded and the musicians had taken their last bow, that the concert had finished, he replied with a sigh: *Endlich!* (At last!)

18. The Instinct for Child-rearing and Pedagogical Instinct

Breathing and Education—Fantasy—Humour—Soccer—
Culture—Music—Teachers as Learners

'Scotland lost again.'
I was teaching in a recently built secondary modern school.
Acres of glass windows, it seemed, cruel, light-stinging
transparency on left and right of the seating in each classroom, all crammed into metal-framed oblongs, with rank
upon rank of strip lighting overhead. I say 'recently built'.
The time lag between occupation and completion allowed
for plenty of finishing touches here and there, which meant
that workmen—and workmen's noises, like intermittent
banging travelling from somewhere far off through the
gurgling plumbing!—were still in evidence. I was allocated
the hall for most lessons where there was a decent piano for
accompanying purposes. There, on more than one occasion,
the class's attention was distracted by a workman descending
in a suspended cage from the stage side of the proscenium
arch (like some *deus ex machina* in an ancient Greek drama)
screwing or drilling or plastering or putting on a final coat of
varnish. There was nothing else one could do in the circumstances except resignedly and mildly enjoy the bizarre
situation along with the pupils.

The job was part-time but there were several classes every
week, each for just one lesson in which, notionally, we sang.
It was in the 50s so the youth of the land were still un-Beatled
and the head teacher's unspoken motto appeared to be

'Culture for the working classes', though one certainly wouldn't put it that way nowadays.

To achieve a modicum of culture, at least musically, I felt that more than just singing was needed, however age-appropriate the songs might have been and apposite for the purpose. I therefore introduced aesthetics to the age 13/14+ youngsters, but in a *very* low key. On one occasion I aimed to get across the idea of variations. I thought the group would be up to following with a modest degree of interest the Brahms *Variations for Orchestra on a Theme of Haydn*, a work whose popularity had stood the test of time.

Even the most unpretentious analysis of musical variations leads you immediately into the basic elements of music: melodic contour, rhythm, harmony, tempo, pitch, structure, key, etc. Demonstrating the last of these, I chose to play a well-known Scottish folk tune, altering its predominantly pentatonic mood by putting it into the minor key and, as I improvised, laying the resulting lugubriousness on a bit thick. Then I asked the class to share impressions. I wasn't expecting a bunch of teenagers from what the head would have called working-class families to break into bubblingly excited responses at this, of course! In fact no one ventured to say anything at all. It was clear some members of the class were churning through their minds as to how to express what were probably unusual feelings, but they were in a minority. I had to assume that the rest were either confused or merely blank, and began contemplating how much longer I should let the stony silence persist. Eventually, bursting the bubble of teenage embarrassment, one boy came up with: 'Scotland lost again!' and I was left to deal with the (not cat) but at least kitten of amusement amongst the pigeons, they being somewhat bemused no doubt with the by now almost unrecognizable folk song that 'Sir' was connecting with 'this bloke called Brahms'.

I wondered if our young 'bringer of jollity' was as bright a spark and as 'fantasy rich' in subjects like science and history or whether it was the cocktail of a teacher in his first teaching post combined with a soft-option subject such as music that brought out the jovial side of his nature. The remark epitomized at once both the finer sentiments that I was trying to evoke and get the pupils to tap into with their awareness as well as the headline-catching culture often associated with soccer—the 50s was well before the sport had become much more than an unbridled and wildly rowdy affair that gobbled up your pocket money on Saturday afternoons while fanning the flames of the cruder feelings that are engendered by alcohol-enhanced rivalry and the carrot-dangling thought of a big win on the pools.

Pedagogically, however, the remark revealed a side of human nature that is just as vital for the teacher to take into account as it is for the pupil to be given *breathing space*. Literally! Just as the body depends on lung and heart, so soul and spirit require the equivalent healthy 'breathing'. However, whilst bodily breathing is a given, the *quality* of which admittedly can be affected by human activity—the fresh-air-fiend approach, the walking-the-dog approach, the avoidance-of-'poison-exuding-paint'-on-the-ceiling approach and so on—soul and spirit 'breathing' depend on human activity. Indeed, it was Steiner's contention that a healthy education, while encouraging an appropriate inhalation/exhalation or contraction/expansion of the soul and spirit, works beneficially on the physiological breathing and thence on the child's general health. Seen in this context, it would not be too much to claim that it therefore becomes part of education's contribution to the adult's effective input in the 'work place', something that might well lead on to such perspectives on life as the 'fulfilling of destiny'.

The whole of Waldorf education can be presented in the light of the above: the way the day is organized by taking the intervening night's sleep into account; the succession of main-lessons during each trimester, those focused more on the inner life (such as maths and grammar) being sandwiched between those that enable the soul-spirit to turn outwards; and in some ways most vital of all, the minute-by-minute pedagogical skills of the *teacher who is teaching*! Thankfully, the further from the Ministry you go and the nearer to the chalk face you get, the more can those pedagogical skills apply, even in the increasingly and oppressively prescriptive curricula and the test-driven, surveillance-dulled, name-and-shame educational 'net' that is being cast ever wider and tighter over our children. That is, one must look for 'signs of best practice' in all sectors of education for they will surely be there, even if stifled in some cases by 'the system'. To whatever extent it is true to say that, over two or three generations, society has lost the instinct for child-rearing, it is similarly true that we cannot count on the 'born teacher'. Steiner insisted that *pedagogical instinct* would be (and certainly would need to be) cultivated.

★　★　★

The 'Scotland lost again' incident is symptomatic of where the contraction/expansion breathing principle is at its most therapeutic. Those who have proliferated the notion of 'laughter is the best medicine' have certainly unearthed a seed of truth in this respect.

We laugh on the out-breath. To be amongst and experience an audience belly-laughing at a clown's pretend trepidation and (even if semi-predictable) ungainly antics on the mini-high-wire can feel almost like an *explosion* of breath. But it is exactly the same phenomenon at the other end of the scale, such as a couple of 'girlies' in the back row of class momentarily tittering at something that has tickled their fancy—the sort of incident where you have to decide whether to step in and nip it in the bud or, more advisedly perhaps, turn a blind eye (especially as it can easily go undetected in a big class: the lips pursed, the eyes dancing together with glee-glances across the intervening space, and the giggling breath forced up from below in little puffs by the 'tittering' diaphragm, escaping through the nostrils with hardly a sound, as the pair in question attempt to conceal their mirth). And there was the extremely macabre case of the tyrant who, during his harangue, lost his dentures as they shot out of his mouth across the courtroom, with the resultant physical agony of the condemned prisoner who *had* to tightly bottle up his instant reaction to go with the guffawing gallery and break into ribald laughter, lest his punishment be advanced from life imprisonment to execution without further trial.

Thus, laughter in all its forms is the physical expression of the soul-spirit's abnormally sudden out-breathing. (We seldom laugh in our sleep!) We also experience the opposite— abnormal in-breathing—in varying degrees: in profuse sobbing, in ritualistic lamentation, in shame, in heart-searching, or in the simple yet acute sadness we feel on hearing of a friend's miscarriage.

It was enough for Steiner if the teacher's light-touch humour elicited nothing more than a *smile in the soul*. Narrative offers the teacher/storyteller fertile opportunities for inducing an artistically moulded oscillation of smiling or sorrowing within the soul. It becomes part of one's 'pedagogical instinct', and therefore clear to the class so that there is no need for concealment, since it is (a) a genuine reaction to the storyteller's art; and (b) what can freely take place within the 'safe space' of the whole group. Such psychological massage also helps to develop in the soul-spirit nature of the growing child that capacity which can go with the inevitable flow of life, but without getting torn towards those extremes (familiar to manic-depressives) that can trespass on and cause havoc in the person's inner equanimity.

★   ★   ★

Earlier, I made the point that breathing of the physical body is a 'given'. By comparison, the kind of soul-spirit breathing that can be set going through good pedagogy is in the teacher's gift—a gift, of course, that by dint of inner effort can be diligently acquired. Not only 'can be acquired', but *needs* to be acquired—ideally in place, even if tentatively, the moment one sets out on a teaching career. It will help ensure that lessons are 'hygienic' as well as everything else they purport to be: imparting knowledge, developing skills, nurturing 'values', cultivating a social sense, assisting the child to go through developmental stages in a fully 'mature' way so that there will be no regrets, recriminations or accumulation of 'unfinished business' that the child will have to take into life as an impediment (like the albatross round the neck of the Ancient Mariner). The thought that education can dissolve such impediments is encouraging. On the other hand, it is salutary to realize that, not altogether dissimilar to the way hospitals have been found to be the harbingers of new and often virile bugs, lifelong burdens can come about through pedagogical malpractice or incompetence.

Fortunately, education is not only a matter of teaching. There are also those who *learn* to be reckoned with! If this is ignored and the teacher falls into an asthmatic mode of teaching (too intensely forcing the students to 'breathe in' the subject matter), it will often happen that the corrective comes from someone in the class. The teacher is not, of course, solely to blame in this most common of pedagogical faults. It can be that he is forced to feel his career is at stake, causing him to fix his sights on promotion and lose sight of the pupils in the process. For example, head teachers not uncommonly step in to boost pupils' achievement, fearing that a dip in their schools' score could lead to personal job loss.* Or, horror of horrors, the Government might bring in a scheme whereby bonuses are paid out linked to exam results, tempting the insufficiently remunerated teacher to pressurize the students into higher achievement. The resultant feeling of oppression in such cases is often 'helped' by the wit of one of the 'sufferers', however annoying the help may seem on the surface to the French 'dragon', or the maths tyrant, or the artist whose head is stuck in the clouds.

The above was a case in point: the incongruency of 22 sweat-stenched soccer players bruising the turf amidst the utter cacophony of rattles and other decibel-marshalling, eardrum-drumming features of the jostling football stadium on the one hand and, beside it, on the other, the 'Bluebells of Scotland' nodding in all their demure delicacy in the sweet, wine-spiced highland air, with the gentle swoosh of wind in the heather and the occasional bird-call to break the silence. The image of the two irreconcilables brought beaming smiles onto the faces of boy and girl alike.

It was one of those occasions when the teacher, if he is

---

* A spokesperson for the National Primary Heads' Association confirmed this view (June 2007): 'When Ofsted comes in, the test scores are the first things inspectors look at.'

sufficiently on the qui vive, is handed on a plate a professional life lesson more potent than anything that can be gained from a book—a new feather in the cap of his pedagogical instinct. There is thus a real chance that though the teacher may find himself from time to time on the Scotland-lost-again side it may turn out to be only a slight and temporary loss of face; and so the victory of the opponents—though it is fatal to even think of the classroom in those terms—will be no more than Pyrrhic!

TEACHER-PUPIL, TEACHER-COLLEAGUE, TEACHER-PARENT RELATIONSHIPS

19. Truth, Beauty and Goodness

Pictorial Thinking and Abstract Rationality—Kindness and
Helpfulness Amongst Peers—Enthusiasm, Training and
Experience—Singing—Rubicon

'. . . every day in all we do'.
Like most teachers, I suppose, in the first days and weeks of
teaching I walked into the classroom with two qualities
standing out in bold relief: a degree of naivety on the one
hand and, on the other, a burning desire to put principles into
practice—all this mixed with a feeling of gratitude towards a
destiny that had opened the doorway for just that.

Naivety is, of course, relative. You can be naive in your
nineties if you find yourself in a completely new situation,
such as being faced with a new computer program with its
possibility of losing a couple of hours' work, or finding
yourself in a totally unfamiliar environment—Mauritania,
say, or Tehran, where you're continually treading on an
unanticipated stretch of thin ice (handling the currency,
etiquette at meals, and so on), or when you become as warily
self-conscious as you are at an auction, freezing your eyebrows when the auctioneer's repartee is at its most lulling and
his hardly discernible survey of the scene is at its most vigilant.

In this instance 'relative' meant new to Waldorf teaching.
The relevance of years and years of teaching—music in a
secondary modern scenario in the 50s, regimental history to
non-commissioned officers in the artillery, country dancing
to deprived children from an inner city district, basketry to
special needs young people, and other professional teaching
situations I had experienced—the relevance of all that

seemed to disappear beyond the present horizon. But the teacher training course under the direction of A.C. Harwood had ignited an enthusiasm for Waldorf, the dousing of which was unthinkable. I was reminded of those first weeks some years later when speaking with an elderly colleague who had gone from class teaching in Edinburgh to mentoring in California. Every evening she would get calls: 'I've done that, Irene. What shall I do tomorrow?' Her eyes sparkled as she reflected: 'Enthusiasm unhindered by experience, I call it!'

As well as class teaching—I had taken over a Class 6 when their teacher left for America—I was time-tabled for singing lessons in the Lower School. My lesson plan with a lively group of 8/9-year-olds (Class 3) included a Bob Copper song about shepherding to go with their farming main-lesson, something redolent of the 'mood of the fifth' in the penta-tonic for those children who were still on the younger side of the Rubicon and, among others, a song with words by Goethe (in translation, of course). This was where my naivety cantered off at full rein.

★   ★   ★

The poem extolled the three fundamental virtues: truth, beauty and goodness. Just right, I thought, start as you intend to go on. Nothing but the best. The other songs in the lesson seemed to fulfil other educational ideals: superb, lifelong nourishing *melodies*, *age-related* subject matter (the Sussex shepherd's song), the liveliness that is needed to address the *sanguinity of childhood*, phrases with a healthy *rhythm*, the possibility of enabling the children to experience so-called *musical form* (something Steiner considered vital right from the first class!), and so on. Now here was something, via an artistic medium (music) that the children would be able to tuck away in the rucksack of their world outlook for future reference during a moment of life reflection or some other pause for thought.

Off we went. They were a musical class, which is not to suggest that there are unmusical classes—but a certain degree of relativity plays in here, too! The tune was catchy. They had it in two or three lessons. Not altogether surprisingly, however, the words were taking longer to learn (at this stage we learnt everything by rote). I wondered why. They didn't seem slow at picking up the words of other songs. Surely there could be no unconscious antipathy towards these three pillars of human conduct: truth, beauty and goodness? And even if there were—unlikely though that was—all the more reason to give the whole notion a good airing, let in some daylight. Especially in this rather musically sugar-coated form. Not at all indoctrinating, of course. The lack of sheer *kindness and helpfulness* amongst peers deplored recently (February 2007) by Professor Jonathan Bradshaw, Professor of Social Policy, University of York, as reported by children who took part in the Unicef research, is not something that can be rammed down the throat. Goodness (truth and beauty too) should dawn from within, not come gatecrashing or pontificating from without.

But I had overlooked the young child's predilection for *pictorial thinking*. More than predilection. Just as water doesn't have a predilection for being wet, so pictorial thinking is an integral part of the young child's nature. I knew it in theory, of course. What's more, I practised it—it was there in all the other songs and, I believed, permeated my pedagogy. It wasn't like some observation of Steiner's on pedagogy to be found in an unexpected context. He did, after all, write umpteen books, let alone give over 6000 lectures which are all extant. Treasures in all these works are to be found in every reading. 'I wish I'd known that before I retired,' commented a greatly valued colleague who had taken on the librarianship of the teachers' library on her retirement, a responsibility which she carried out into her 90s. As I enthused about one of Steiner's pedagogical observations when returning a library book, she revealed that her vocational enthusiasm remained unabated—in her very bones. No, this was no abstruse remark handed down the generations from a private conversation some decades after it had been made. On the contrary, had Steiner been a pulpit-thumper his oft-repeated 'teach in pictures' would have readily resounded in that category.

Teaching in pictures is the lifeblood of pedagogy, especially to children in the Lower School, though naturally the degree of pictorial self-sufficiency tapers as *rational thought* begins its process of awakening. It's not a matter of box-ticking, like making an announcement, calling the register, or ensuring that each individual knows the 7 × multiplication table and suchlike. *Have I remembered to teach in pictures?* If your teaching is not imbued with this basic pedagogical principle, then you're likely to be in for learning a lesson as well as giving one.

On this occasion, by about the fourth singing lesson, the children's voices began to sound less diffident. I made some complimentary remark and sensed there would be no reticence in singing the song again. A little 'intro' from me at the piano and we were song-borne. In fact, the mood of 'less diffidence' quickly started spilling over into gusto. My accompaniment accordingly became more florid—a kind of must-keep-up-with-the-Jones's creeping in. If I'd allowed myself to be completely carried away, to the tune of not really hearing what the children were singing, my reprobation might never have happened. I would still to this day be under some such illusion as: Good ol' Goethe; no need to bother whether his immortality is clad in child-friendliness.

For, as the chorus got louder in each verse, positively raucous by the end of the song, I realized that instead of singing 'Goodness, truth and beauty heeding, / Every day in all we do', which is how the translation expressed the concept (what on earth is 'heeding' to an 8-year-old? I should have asked myself), the class had capriciously supplemented my momentary lapse in 'teach in pictures' and were revelling at the tops of their voices with: 'Goodness, truth and *central heating . . .*'

Wistfully licking my wounds some decades later, I'm wondering whether a teacher's songbook might not be worth publishing for future training courses with a soupçon of spoof Goethe to liven up the training: 'Waldorf teachers: *teach in pictures* / Every day in all you do'.

20. Dross and Gold in the Four Temperaments

Education and Interest—Boredom—'Drink, Drugs and Sex'—Teaching and *Learning*—Therapeutic Verses for Children

'He's bone idle.'

The pompous but redoubtable Regimental Sergeant Major of the Coldstream Guards (Ronald Britain) could occasionally be heard to make this remark during one's short stay at the officer cadet training unit in Aldershot, while serving the two years of National Service in the period following the Second World War. The words were always the culmination of a little melodrama. Every two weeks there would be a Passing Out Parade, and in the interim a rehearsal took place. Through this you gradually crept your way—crept with much boot- and soul-destroying 'square-bashing', of course—to the 'front of the queue'. And, providing it was not your misfortune to *pass out*—and it was by no means unheard of for someone to go down like a log onto the tarmac, bayoneted rifle stiffly in hand, the ultimate disgrace—you would *Pass Out* and be posted to your next unit fighting fit for (simulated active, or dreary day-languishing inactive) service.

The parades themselves were immaculate examples of military ritual, in which the will has been tempered to act snappily at the word of command, bypassing emotion and any trace of autonomous thought. The sergeant major's little melodramas occurred only at rehearsals. They were usually over some hardly discernible fault in the cadet's turnout: a spot of Brasso left undetected on the blancoed belt for instance. Undetected by the unmotivated cadet, that is, but pounced on by the eagle eyes of the RSM (Regimental Sergeant Major), who was always ready to enliven the inordinately dull mood of the occasion, far from the field of battle, with the odd 'storm in a teacup'—or if circumstance demanded, or dullness had reached an all-time low: tornado in a thimble!

The procedure was that each cadet's gear was scrutinized—the absolute polar opposite to the sauntering unconcern usually displayed by the supreme commander on the day itself. The RSM was accompanied in the act of inspection by another sergeant major who was there to do his bidding and add psychological Yorkshire pudding to the already imposing six-foot-something beef of the RSM. The flaw in your equipment having been detected, the fuse of his fill-the-parade-ground voice would instantly fizz, and the preposterousness of your having betrayed your Queen and country by being turned out in this slovenly fashion would explode over you like a cannon ball shot from the barrel of some piece of Napoleonic artillery. Expletives were usually unnecessary—though not unknown—for the *tone* of voice said it all. And as if that were not enough, with the whole event of course being deeply inscribed in the Akashic Record (!), the final ignominy would volcano forth: *Take his name Sergeant Major!* And if you were very, very lucky—the splodge of Brasso, perhaps, having been detectable from a yard away and not a mere nose-pinched, scrutinizing six inches—the legend come true would reach its Armageddon: 'He's not idle [dramatic pause as his plenteous moustache bristled on the pouted upper lip and his top-brassed cap-peak was thrust an inch and a half skywards]: he's *bone* idle.'

★   ★   ★

So much in Steiner's approach to pedagogy is awakening—
be it towards positive enlightenment or strong scepticism—
because it turns the past through 180 degrees. For most
people the notion of a person's *temperament* is that of a
negative trait in the character. *Sanguine*: a butterfly, lacking
concentration, unreliable, out of touch with life. *Choleric*:
bloody-minded, bludgeoning his way egotistically, insensi-
tively through all the social hoops. *Melancholic*: miserable as
sin. And *phlegmatic*: bone idle. Steiner exhorted the teacher
(especially in the Lower School) to take the temperament
seriously into her pedagogy every moment of the day. Instead
of dismissing the whole subject as a light-hearted medieval
diversion—or worse, something that went out of fashion
with the decline of ancient Greece—consider the temperament of each child personally and imbue one's teaching with
methods that address, appeal to, engage and harness the virtues of the temperament.

Virtues? Bone-idleness, misery, egotism and unrelia-
bility...! Whatever did Steiner have in mind?

These undesirables, which undoubtedly are connected
with temperament, are the qualities we commonly attach to a
person's temperamental behaviour. But *temperamental* is the
'black sheep' of the family—alchemically *temperamental dross*,
which most of us know only too well if we are honest with
ourselves. It was Steiner's contention that each person is born
as much with their own temperament as with their own
physical bodily constitution. We can look after our physical
body, in terms of health, hygiene and nutrition, thus averting
illness. With the temperament we can be more proactive—
not merely 'look after it' but make efforts to turn the dross
into gold. Temperamental dross becomes *temperament gold*

through inner effort—an ego activity. Through such activity the self-indulgent misery of the melancholic becomes deep understanding and sympathy towards the other unfortunate. The losing-the-thread-of-thought nature of the sanguine becomes the ability to bring opposites together, to come up spontaneously and effortlessly with the right word, the right gesture, the right action in any situation, however unforeseen. The inertia of the phlegmatic becomes unflappability, dependability, order and organizational prowess. And the off-the-leash egotism of the choleric becomes the fire of enthusiasm that combines drive with consideration for others. There are allied virtues, too, which we need not spell out here.

If this were all that there was to Steiner's view of the child's nature, it would lay itself open to the danger of compartmentalizing each child into a *stereotype*. This kind of danger was highlighted recently when the Director of the charity Act Against Bullying objected to the 'Billy Bunter' type of story that presented a stereotype which could easily offend some (plump) children whose natures were anything but bullies: 'It would be nice to . . . see the *individuality* in one another rather than the stereotype.' Unquestionably true. Nevertheless, it is equally true that each individuality manifests his or her own version of the temperament. (Not totally dissimilar are the categories of one building being a Greek temple and another being a Gothic cathedral, which in no way removes the temple's or the cathedral's unique character.) It is vital not to lose sight of the rich complexity of human nature.

★   ★   ★

In childhood, the ego is in its prolonged human state of incarnating. To expect it to take full control of the inner aspects of life which the temperament bears within itself—

converting the temperamental negatives and cultivating the temperamental positives—would be to risk burdening the whole of its development. The teacher, therefore, takes on board the ego responsibility but in such a way that does not marginalize the child's ego or weaken it through neglect, but draws it into the alchemical process in an appropriate way. This means that there is a good chance that the best forces of the person can come through in adulthood less hindered by temperamental counterweights.

As Steiner set such store on this happening during the Lower School phase of education, there are many examples of how to work positively with the temperament in his educational writings: how to use the 'four operations' in *arithmetic* (plus, minus, divide, multiply); how to use the different categories of *musical instruments* (wind, strings, percussion and harmony instruments); different shapes in *form drawing*; various uses of *colour* (so that the complementary colour is brought into play); images in *storytelling* (in the way landscapes for example are described, such as the eruption of a volcano, the solitude of dark forests, the peak-aspiring mountain ranges, the peace and quiet of sky-reflecting lagoons and lakes); *annually written verses* that the individual temperament can recite each week; and so on.

Pervading the whole of teaching at this phase of child-hood, however, is the deeper principle of what is actually therapeutic for the temperament. This is an area where misunderstandings occur. We are not balancing *out* the temperament. The gold that was formerly dross is still the same temperament gold. Worse still is the frequently mis-taken concept that we *change* the temperament. Who would want to change from an unreliable sanguine into a des-perately introverted melancholic? Heaven forbid! Although there are subtle differences between the child's and the adult's temperament, *the temperament remains the same.* We are born with it and retain it for life despite other members of our nature that may overlay or even semi-eclipse the temperament. And the difference between child and adult we are then concerned with is that of changing the situation whereby the temperament becomes a strongly influential component, which can be seen in the child's behaviour, to the adult temperament, which becomes a tool in the hands of the ego—a useful, life-enhancing, well-maintained tool, not one that is dysfunctional.

In the wake of that educational journey (child to adult), the four different temperaments have *inherent interests.* Most of us would find more than a grain of truth in the old adage 'the devil makes work for idle hands'—*his* work needless to say. It is not a Captain-Armstrong-step-on-the-moon from there to considering the slippery slope the devil gleefully lards for bored schoolchildren. The three dis-graces (*drink, drugs and underage sex*) could hardly get more media coverage than at present. We don't need to look at the statistics for binge drinking, substance abuse and teenage pregnancies to flag that there must be a vacuum in the souls of young people, causing them to get drawn into such questionable outlets. And it is no argument to point out that SATS (Standard Attainment Tests) and all the rest of our educational surveillance culture prevent their hands from being idle. We cannot do away with the quantitative, of course, but if lessons lack lustre and qualitatively creative teaching, piling on the test-driven culture with which we flog our children is likely to prove counter-productive. In the SATS-free zone of Waldorf education, and knowing the vital importance of engendering interest, the teacher broaches her subject via the temperaments, each one in turn.

The observations of Dr Andrew Curran, consultant

neurologist at Alder Hey Hospital, Liverpool, speaking at the Learning Brain Conference in Oxford this year (2007) when he emphasized the importance of appreciation and interest in the classroom ethos, help to explain this. When such an ethos is engendered, dopamine rushes to the brain causing the brain cells to reach out and connect—the so-called Hebbian effect. The opposite prevails in an atmosphere of humiliation, where steroids are produced that kill nerve cells in the hippocampus, that part of the brain associated with memory.

Let us take a seemingly mundane example. Interest in the county of Kent, whose reputation as the 'Garden of England' the teacher is wanting to get across, is roused in different ways. Hearing the description of the sweet juice of a ripe rosy apple will harmonize with the phlegmatic's healthy lymphatic system. The fluttering of cherry blossom and later its fruit dangling in the bird-excited branches will gladden the sanguine's inner eye. The sharpening of saw teeth, when pruning time in the huge orchards comes round each year, and the setting fire to the 'rubbish' will rouse the choleric's sense of purpose and activity on a grand scale. The danger of late frosts and the necessity of combating these, or of drought, will draw forth the melancholic's anxiety.

As the teacher weaves and wends through such aspects of fruit-growing, which appeal specially to each temperament, not only is the interest of *that* temperament quickened, but the other three temperaments sense it sufficiently to be gently drawn into the current of interest that thus flows throughout the teacher's presentation of the subject. And interest, of course, is one of the most important keys to *learning*. Unless it is there from the beginning or evoked, the teacher can teach till she is blue in the face—but without much chance of enriching the soul in her students and thereby preventing the danger of boredom slithering into the devil-delighting extremes which are on the conscience of both educationist and parent.

Knowledge of the temperament is thus not only of great help to the child's inner development, it greatly assists learning; and for the teacher (a very practical consideration) it reduces a possible unwieldly large class into four very manageable groups. In an un-ideal world it will not obliterate other measures that the teacher will have to take, e.g. the phlegmatic who still is occasionally bone idle. But in the battle of modern life, cultivating the temperament pedagogically will undoubtedly provide the ego, as it deploys its cadet-like faculties, with a better weapon than it otherwise would have had.

21. The Oft-ignored Ingredient in School Readiness

Formal Schooling—Cut-off Date for Entry into Class 1—
Septennial Phases—Paternity in the Home—
Metamorphosis—Finland and the Pisa Study

'I'm tired.'

I only heard of the above remark the day after the incident had occurred. A colleague had found a boy from my class reclined on the grass, one warm sunny autumn day after school. It was mid-afternoon. 'I'm tired,' was his simple response to her 'What are you doing...?' It was at the end of the very first day of Class 1. At that time the school's policy for entry into the first class was such that he had come up from the Kindergarten with the rest of the group, even though he was not yet six. Over the next few years the cut-off date was revised—brought back some months closer to where it was in Steiner's day—but this boy had somehow slipped through the net. One could see why. He was as bright as a button—two buttons at times! Lithesome with it, too. One could imagine him, for all his niceness, being a will-o'-the-wisp in the Kindergarten—a handful, though often anywhere but 'in hand'. The parents saw his 'acceptance' into Class 1 as a sign that he would shin up the ladder of success with flying colours. This being the case, I don't know what they made of his small frame slumped in the arms of my matronly-looking colleague, appearing on the doorstep, with his cheeks paler than usual. It was, however, the first and last time anything like that had happened and our conversations during home visits and at other times did not make or require any reference to the incident, the button-brightness in his character remaining seemingly untarnished.

For me, however, that first day of Class 1 lived on. Isolated though it has been in my teaching experience—either before or since—I have often wondered what was at work. Surely, though exceptional, and indeed unique, it must have been something to do with Steiner's perception about *formal learning*, and the appropriate time in child development to have expectations of the child in this regard. Every educationist who is at all aware of Steiner's clear perspective will cite his insistence on the septennial phases of childhood as being of importance in the child's development. The matter of school readiness hinges entirely on the changeover from the first seven years of life to the second, though this is not to imply that the change suddenly takes place like an alarm clock going off.

★ ★ ★

In Steiner's day a relaxed attitude towards school readiness was not such an issue. It was virtually standard practice to see the *home* as the ideal setting for the first seven years—ideal, that is, from the point of view of informal learning, such factors as the virtual nonexistence of *paternity leave*, advocated recently (March 2007) by the Equal Opportunities Commission, notwithstanding. Radical changes in social life, exacerbated through the two World Wars, had the knock-on effect that children were placed in kindergarten prior to formal schooling. From there it was not a rocket-science leap to 'prepare' children for school already in the kindergarten. All this, despite any residual instinct that people may have had regarding healthy child raising and, ironically enough, despite the German slogan associated with the 30s that the woman's place in society was bound up with *children*, with the *kitchen* and with *religion* (*Kinder, Küche, Kirche*)—a view hardly even quotable these 'politically correct' days except in a purely and tightly restricted historic context.

And so it went on. Did we even realize what a threatening slope education was slithering down, until the figures from Finland that surfaced in the 2003 Pisa study showed the educational world at the beginning of the millennium what a state it had got itself into? The best education results were obtained from a country—everyone suddenly realized— which had retained its adherence to school readiness being a standard *seven* years of age. It is not only Finland that appreciated this aspect of child development. Sue Palmer, author of *Toxic Childhood: How Modern Life is Damaging Our Children and What We Can Do About It*, recently reported a conversation she had had with Dutch teachers who were horrified at the 'cruel' practice of *early formal learning* in the UK. The outspoken head teacher thought that 'you Anglo-Saxons are mad'. The Dutch, it should be noted here, scored highest in the Unicef report and did almost as well as the Finns under the heading of education.

But despite anecdotes and the Pisa research being so thoroughly investigated we are still waiting to see if the findings are going to rock the boat or, more importantly, if they will affect the course that educationists are steering towards. A canoe or kayak must be the most navigable of all forms of water transport. But the systems adopted by and entrenched in so many western countries of *formal* early years learning must be about as flexible in their manoeuvrability as an aircraft carrier! Moreover, the passengers in the aircraft—if we extend the metaphor—continue to be, in the main, subject to formal learning even with an increasing amount of *pressure* in their first seven years.

It is not clear whether the successful 'protection' of the first seven years in the Finnish system is the result of a healthily lingering folk instinct for what is right or whether to any extent there has been some Steiner influence corroborating perhaps that instinct. Professor Reijo Wilenius, a one-time teacher in the Helsinki Steiner School, was certainly a highly respected authority in government circles. His book published in 1964 on *Society and Education* was appreciated by the then Minister of Education, Johannes Virolainen, who is attributed with having begun steering the education system towards its present prestigious position. It is also acknowledged that the respect for Wilenius's views regarding various aspects of cultural life was a significant factor in the laws passed in 1977 and 1991, which specifically supported Steiner schools. Similarly, a law passed in 2002 led to the recognition and State funding of Snelman College in Helsinki, where Steiner teacher training and other adult courses based on Steiner's research takes place. This suggests that five factors are, if not provenly interlinked, certainly to be seen as part of the same cultural scenario:

(i) Finnish mainstream education according to the Pisa report is unsurpassed elsewhere;

(ii) the first seven years of childhood are not encroached upon by early learning;

(iii) the Finns' way of life is highly supportive of children (the Unicef report);

(iv) Steiner education at all levels—Kindergarten, Lower School, Upper School and Further Education—is recognized by the State as being an important contribution to the country's cultural life;

(v) the density of Steiner schools per capita is one of the highest in the world.

I am leaving on one side the fact that Wilenius had *teaching experience* at both school and FE level. He is not regarded as a 'political animal'.

However, though empirically justified (it works, Finnish schools have come out 'top'), one wonders whether the academic and political *will* is sufficiently motivated to enquire deeply into the whys and wherefores, as the waves caused by contemporary research wash onto other political shores. Particularly is this the case in that, though results are measurable at the intellectual level, the cause, if we follow Steiner's perceptions, lies elsewhere. Though we polish up our logic to whatever prized and dazzling degree we like, without the concept of intrinsic *metamorphosis* we will be unlikely to arrive at an understanding of what is taking place. And without *understanding* conviction will be unlikely to ensue; and without *conviction* the old laissez-faire is likely to steamroller on with the inevitable effect of numbed alertness and continued unchecked damage. If it isn't the quagmire of inertia that is perpetuating the UK's deplorable record vis-à-vis 'lost childhood', as the leader in *The Daily Telegraph* (14 November 2006) put it, what is it?

★   ★   ★

Hence to *metamorphosis*. Though it is so obvious that we hardly take note of it, the life in the physical body is an entity that has its own functions and rhythms—*a life of its own*. The function of growth stares us in the face, especially if we are going through puberty and agonize about or gloat over what we see reflected in the bathroom mirror! The function of recycling hits the headlines from time to time: stem cells in the spleen or in the liver. We read the function of regencration on a scale from zero (hip replacement, say) to ten (the daily grind of shaving!). The function of life itself, apart from any adrenaline-fed *joie de vivre* that we may enjoy from time to time, is perhaps at its most evident, paradoxically, when gone for ever—as we follow the funeral hearse. But there is one function of the life forces which is peculiar to the first seven years: the *shaping* of the physical form. Two eyes, a nose and a mouth—yes, of course—but what shape do they have? And how much inherent strength resides in the overall form of each growing child's physical body?

As Steiner saw it, it is this last function of metamorphosis which, once its task is complete—one of the signs that this is so being the eruption of the permanent teeth—becomes the capacity for learning (to put it broadly). Induce formal learning before that task has been completed and one risks encroaching on that particular function of the life forces. Some early learning will undoubtedly take place, of a kind (IQ measurable) that would not otherwise be the case, but— as the research which put Finland at the top suggests—it will be at the expense of those very faculties one is seeking to advance through early learning. Put colloquially, being forced into running before you can walk will result in weaker running. (I sometimes find myself wondering what repercussions this counter-productive practice—surely not policy?—has in the international sport scene . . .)

I was reminded of the vital importance—would sacredness be too strong a word?—of nurturing and protecting these early-years life forces on an occasion when speaking to the Parent-Teacher Association of one of the London Waldorf schools. It occurred like a flashback. A babe in arms had been crying. One of the class teachers offered to go out of the room with the baby so that the mother could concentrate on the lecture, and at the exact point where I arrived at the importance of nurturing the life forces during the first seven years the teacher, who had been successful in rocking the baby back to sleep, walked back into the hall to return him to his mother. It was at that moment that I realized she was that *same* colleague (now teaching in a different school) who, in those *same* arms, had 'delivered' to his thankful parents their son—bordering on the young side for Class 1—tired and stretched out in the autumn sun some 20 years earlier!

In medieval times, such a profound inner gesture would surely have found its outer representation somewhere on a knight's escutcheon!

22. Teacher-Pupil Pedagogical Relationships

Classroom Management—Spectator Consciousness—
Mentoring—Judgement in Childhood—Mixed Ability—
Collegial Interest in Research—Staying-on Records

'You can't teach like that.'
A medical doctor friend had been in the 'top' class of the first Waldorf school. His admiration for and indefatigable study of Steiner's work continued throughout his entire life. His insight into the nature of illness was broad and deep and the workload he retained until into his eighties was awe-inspiring. Yet a lifelong study of spiritual science backing up his powers of healing had not blunted his memories of what it was like to be a teenager. Far from it! Once he recounted an incident that had occurred in what must have been Class 11 or 12—I suspect the latter, as it demonstrates how Steiner could rely on the *maturing judgement* of pupils at school-leaving age (18/19 years if one includes the 'exam preparation' class).

As was his wont, Steiner would visit classes in the school during his fairly regular times in Stuttgart, often en route from Switzerland to other parts of Europe. Dr Hermann von Baravalle was teaching an Upper School maths main-lesson. He was an outstanding mathematician—Steiner's admiration for him came out forcibly in a teachers' meeting on one occasion when he urged the entire teaching staff to read Baravalle's doctoral thesis. His nimble wizardry with numbers can still be savoured in early Waldorf publications. The pupils

also clearly admired the man's competence in his subject—
and one should bear in mind that the remit of the main-
lesson teacher is to teach the *whole* class, no simple task in
advanced mathematics to a group who, by definition, will be
of considerably mixed ability. In Class 12 this will especially
be the case since it will entail touching on the kind of
specialized topics in each subject that would be on a par with
an A-level syllabus. It is a natural consequence of the Waldorf
maxim that a broad curriculum should not *at the same time*
result in or resort to superficiality, but rather depth of
understanding (be it in history or architecture, philosophy or
whatever). It is even arguable that the presence of pupils in a
group who have a hard time chewing over something might
of itself increase the nutritive value of that something for
those numeracy-gluttons who would otherwise make short
work over mentally digesting it.

Be that as it may, during the main-lesson in question
Steiner sat on one side observing, and at a certain point
interrupted Baravalle with no less than: 'You can't teach like
that!' (*Nicht kann man so unterrichten!*) I don't recall our
medical friend saying how incisive the interruption was—
heralded by an 'Ahem!' or flying across the room like a
tomahawk . . . Comment as to that, in any case, would have
been superfluous, the situation being that here was one of the
young people's admired teachers—the age when you are
seeking (*needing*) role models—being criticized publicly by
the person whom everyone around acknowledged as *the*
outstanding teacher of the age on so many levels, both personal and corporate.

Something that you would expect an orthodox handbook
to say should *never ever* happen. However, in this case—and it
reflects the genius of both Baravalle and Steiner—his being
criticized did *not*, in our friend's estimation, mean taken

down a peg in his relationship with the class, i.e. with their perception of him. The psychology involved here is complex. It certainly incorporates an unshakeable element of trust and respect between teacher and pupil—an ethos that one imagines Lord Falconer, the Lord Chancellor, would have given his wig for when, in view of the increasing number of deliberately false allegations of teachers assaulting pupils, he recently proposed that schools protect the *anonymity* of teachers!

Examining the remarks Steiner made in the teachers' meeting—these are extant and were published under the title *Die Konferenzen*—as mentioned above, one finds that he makes, or implies, a special distinction between teaching and lecturing. (I am slightly interpreting.) Whilst in lecturing it is conceivable (indeed, likely) that the bulk of a 'public' audience is unknown to the lecturer, in teaching it is imperative that *the teacher constantly keep in touch with each pupil*. Steiner, clearly adopting the principle of building on what was positive, seldom reprimanded teachers; but he was known to do so strongly if they got taken up with their subject in such a way that crucial pupil contact was lost, however temporarily.

★ ★ ★

It's a perfectly understandable and familiar situation to any Upper School teacher. The very presence of eager-minded teenagers eggs you on to share your research, your premeditated thoughts, even *further* them, on the spur of the moment—the kind of 'diversion' where the pupils readily perceive that (whatever your age!) you are still young at heart and enquiring in spirit. It's at such times that the line between getting wound up in your subject and keeping in touch with where the students are at can get blurred. Admittedly, the line often becomes as thin as thin can be in good Upper

School teaching, but let the teacher become lost in his cloud—and it doesn't have to be a puffed-up, egoistic cloud of self-aggrandizement—and the last shred of contact disappears. If a parallel situation occurs in personal conversation, politely one might say: 'You've lost me there.' A class of pupils can usually only convey that kind of message silently; and on the occasion in question Steiner clearly considered Baravalle wasn't listening to the silence.

This kind of situation occurs with the currently highlighted case of the so-called 'invisible child'. It is on a smaller scale, of course, with the teacher being in danger of overlooking the child because of the demanding behaviour of others in the class—attention-seeking pupils, 'bright sparks' whose hands are always eagerly shooting up, behavioural problems of one kind or another and so on—than getting lost in his own subject. There is the potential knock-on effect that such a child, together with those whose interest the teacher has failed to stimulate, will not stay on beyond the statutory age.

David Miliband, when he became schools minister in the UK in 2002, described the staying-on record (beyond school leaving) as a 'shame and disgrace'. Particularly in view of the fact that apprenticeships were held in high esteem (a strong German trait), the Waldorf school in the 1920s achieved a remarkable staying-on record. Judging by the profound appreciation and fondness with which Baravalle was held in our friend's memory he must have been one of the reasons behind this. Steiner's decision to openly criticize his pedagogical fault in a way that wouldn't upset the pupils' relationship with their teacher must have been a bold yet correct one, with Steiner relying on Baravalle rallying rather than reeling!

★   ★   ★

The incident is in some senses a one-off. But it highlights what can be a common experience: witnessing a colleague teach—as student-teacher on a school visit, as mentor attending week by week her mentee's lessons as is usually and wisely the case during the first year of a new appointment, as pianist who is playing for a eurythmy lesson witnessing the eurythmist's pedagogical skills (perhaps one of the most sensitive of examples), and so on. Of course, we live in a 'spectator' age: tens of thousands watching (and paying handsomely to watch) 30 mud-splattered men viciously chasing, kicking the guts out of, hurling themselves with bodily fury upon, snatching with all their aggressive might, disputing and on the verge of coming to blows with the referee over . . . an 'innocent' rugby ball! However, we don't need such extremes to be reminded of the far-apartness of the two worlds of consciousness: that of the 'witness' and that of the 'performer'.

In exercising two layers of consciousness at once, the teacher brings her 'performing art' (if I may put it that way) into close juxtaposition with the spectator-consciousness of self. This will entail being acutely aware and ready to pounce appropriately in classroom management situations, ebullient when it comes to subtly directing class discussion times, and calmly, owl-staringly watchful during her own presentation of subject matter—and hence conscious, without lull, of the inner voice: 'You can't/*can* teach like that!'

23. Will Activity

Communication—Confidentiality—Early Years—
Temperaments—Nutrition—Adolescent Behaviour—
Mass-production—An Indictment of Society

'I'm allowed.'

It was a very orderly queue, stretching almost out into the street. But as the shop had a lengthy glassed-in passage area decked out for the display of wares, it meant you could wait under shelter before you got to your turn at the counter. The long narrow passage also ensured that no queue-jumping was possible, so once you were in the queue you bided your time, waited your turn, admired the crafts on display and, as like as not, engaged in conversation with other customers.

As the shop was near a Waldorf school and was the first 'village' retailer to sell organic and biodynamic food, trade was brisk. So the lengthy queue was to be expected, which meant that on occasion conversations could become deep— heated even. Parents would occasionally forget the very public space in which they were, and express strong opinions or even let fall a confidentiality. One of the most sensitive organizational areas of any institution is communication. Is it enough? Is it in the right form? Is the message getting across? Who needs to be told what? And often the most important: Who needs to be told *first*? Then there is the constant battle between 'too little, too late' on the one hand, and too oft-repeated, causing communications fatigue on the other. So, all in all, a queue in such circumstances is not at all what we think of as the epitome of British phlegm, such as when passengers stand uncomplainingly in the drizzle for their bus.

Infinitely worse must have been the mood of grey hope-lessness amongst Soviet citizens when they were forced to wait in yet another queue for some scarce commodity—the result of an economy grinding to a halt, now thankfully consigned to history books and doleful memories.

In such circumstances—and I am deliberately only inching my way forward with this tale—with ears all around on the alert and in the fascination of voices condensing into spasms of hushed guardedness or exploding into guffaws of laughter, a queue becomes something of an orchestra of sound and interest, being mesmerized by which it is easy temporarily to lose track of where your 'terrible' two-year-old has got to. Which is exactly what happened on a busy Saturday morning one wet autumn day. Some of the children in tow had got together and formed happy little clusters, semi-blocking the exit route of the long passage. But the resourceful two-year-old was not one of them, a fact which the customers became forcefully aware of as the parent's lapse of consciousness resulted in his adventurous son finding a new source of delight: a huge tub of shelled hazelnuts—huge beside a two-year-old. It must have been a recent delivery, for the nuts almost filled it to the brim. *The brimful tub of hazelnuts . . .* this sets the stage for the little one-act drama that ensued.

Suddenly there were showers of nuts, like some newly created plague of Egypt, pelting down from the ceiling on the very unsuspecting shoppers. The parent was so deep in his philosophical conversation that it took him some moments to become aware that hazelnuts were actually littering him from above, and that the blunderbussing was the result of his very own son's pent up need for activity, causing confusion all around. The standers-by of course, were thrust into a real quandary. What were they to do about this chubby little gyroscope of delighted two-year-old fury, hurling fists-full of dark brown nuts into suburbia? The melancholics looked troubled and wondered to whom he 'belonged'. The sanguines' eyes creased with amusement at the whole scene. The phlegmatics did their best to dodge the descending debris without losing too much aplomb. The cholerics, always at the ready, attempted to stop the bombardment by exercising instant bodily restraint. That was the worst! Junior's voice rose to town-crier proportions: 'I'm allowed. I'm allowed!' he informed the universe. At this, the proprietress, a woman who had raised a family of four herself, appeared on the scene, summed it up in a flash, took one of the nut-crammed fists in her experienced gentle grasp and cajoled: 'Let's go upstairs and have a look at...' This one wave of the wand was all that was needed. Junior followed the 'shepherdess' like a lamb. The parent stood aghast, obviously filled with admiration, whilst the excited commentators on the scene gradually resumed their composure and recalled their train of thought. The cheese-wire went on cutting. The scales continued their infallible task of revealing measured truth. The labels on packets affirmed once more 'Demeter' for quality. And the carpet of hazelnuts was harvested for some sort of treatment by a member of staff looking, as I recall it, rather fraught.

★   ★   ★

Adolescents with not enough to inspire them will, most likely, subside into doldrums of inner heaviness or burst into some sort of antisocial extravagance. We know it only too well. Arguably, adolescents have been a pain in the neck of society for generations. But the 'bad and risky' adolescent behaviour (flaunted in public under-age sex, drugs, etc.) which is now being lambasted as an indictment of society itself hardly bears comparison any more with the sowing of wild oats that, however irksome, was a more or less accepted phase through which youth passed as part of its rite of passage. 'Depressing and alarming,' commented Martin Barnes, Chief Executive of the charity Drugscope recently. Unlike wild oats, however, a two-year-old has no such inner escape routes. The early years as a whole, in fact, come under the star of *will*, of activity, of *experiential learning*. An imperceptibly moving queue of adults wrapped up in conversation or standing seemingly idle is anathema to such a two-year-old, where the accent of psychological development is on the will.

Although Waldorf Kindergartens only came into their own after Steiner's death, it was clear from his exposition of child development what aspect in the child's nature would be the foundation for all early years' work. In his view of the child, the corollary to the bodily develop-ment—where emphasis is on the nerve-senses in the first seven years, going on to the rhythmic system in the second seven years, and the maturation of the metabolic, repro-ductive and limb systems in the post-puberty years—was that the child's psychological connections with the world followed the polar opposite direction. When we talk about growing up, and if we are referring to physical growth, the 'up' is, in fact, the result of growing *down*, the growth start-ing in the head, proceeding to the trunk and ending with the limbs. In the days when school uniform was far more prevalent, the school cap eventually lasted a boy quite some time. Thus by age 16 it was usually in a disreputable state (and the more disreputable, the prouder you felt!), whereas shoes became too tight before they had had time to wear out. We are nearer to the truth when we admonish a bolshy 14-year-old (if we take that line) with 'Grow up!' meaning that we appeal to and depend on his hopefully awakening thoughtfulness, consideration and sense of responsibility, etc. Often a long haul!

Yet one might say that there is no such thing as an uninspired, two-year-old *will*. It's as if will itself—if it is uninhibited, unadulterated, unsuppressed—is the very bearer of creativity and inspiration. Hamlet, who couldn't bring himself to act on the increasingly convincing evidence of his stepfather's having murdered his father, was imprisoned in his thinking. Not until the end of the play are the floodgates of the will tragically flung open. Of course, the adult, in the main, needs to give balanced thought to her actions. The younger generation, on the other hand, can count on a sufficiently healthy connection with the will, so to say, that they cannot do anything wrong. Inconvenient, yes, which means that socially there's often a steep learning curve. Flinging fistfuls of sand into the air, if you're the only one on the beach, as a paean of gratitude to Nature for her bounty feels exhilarating—and no doubt Nature will share in the exhilaration. But those hazelnuts...?

This does not mean, of course, that the world is so organized that it is in total harmony with this. Cut glass that can break, toilet-cleaning chemicals that can poison, long flights of stairs that can be fallen down not only by the accident-prone, sockets in the wall that can electrify, and a dozen other hazards are simply part of everyday life. And we are often unable to assign such hazards to the safety of high shelves, well out of reach of our two-year-old.

These are dangers to life and limb with which an uninhibited early years' child could easily be enthralled. There are, however, less obvious hazards that are almost unavoidable in modern life. Mechanical egg whisks, even if not powered electrically, do not offer the young child's will forces the same freedom of movement as an example for imitation as does a

simple utensil which necessitates beating the eggs until they
are the required texture. Similarly, with many objects that
surround us—the curtains we hang, the chairs we sit on, the
cars we drive in, the brushes we sweep with—they are mostly
mass-produced and thus, through being identically churned
out, are one step removed from the creativity and inventive
design that went into them in the first place. (Steiner appears
to have considered mass-produced music as the end of the
road in this respect.) So the fantasy of children, which is
deeply connected to the life forces in their nature, is sur-
rounded with domestic objects that disclose a machine finish
rather than that of the *hand* that would have been evident in
similar objects in a less industrial age. What a world of difference there is between what we mean by *hand made* and
what we mean by its Latin twin, *manufactured* (*manus* = hand;
facto = made). The will of the 0/7-year-old belongs to the
former world. Today even our dwelling places tend to be
'standard' sizes, despite all the tweaks we give to the positioning of windows or staircases. There is a multitude of
choices with which we are confronted when we open a
manufacturer's catalogue: door frames, window panes, curtain materials, floor tiles, fireplaces, radiators, showers, sinks,
cat-flaps, fitted cupboards in the kitchen, up and over doors
in the garage, and so on. These and our multiples-of-four-
by-two rooms are often dominated by the all-convenient
right-angle. The eye of a child resting on the commonest of
double storey, gable-ended external brick walls with, say,
one window up and down, will 'see' the three angles of a
triangle in the gable, but otherwise about 2000 (*sic*) right
angles, no less! Such common percepts are part of modern
life, not the life of a nomadic Kazakhstani whose dwelling
place less than a century ago was a yurt made of felted camel
hair, or that of an American Indian in his reserve. But

manufactured! What a misnomer, as far as the ever-active, ever-adventurous, ever-learning, experientially-inspired *will* of a young child is concerned—part of 'life', yet at the same time increasingly lifeless.

★   ★   ★

All the above is not cause for gloom and despondency on the assumption that the will of young children is doomed by the world that the West has created, and therefore the basis upon which further development is built during the rest of life is inadequate, flawed from the beginning, etc. It *is*, however, cause for pedagogical alertness. From time to time the role of *movement* in education does surface on the agenda. In Derby this summer (2007), for instance, a thousand State schools are being fitted with sensors which will record and monitor the movements of children in reception and year 6. (The media attention that the 'move' attracted seemed largely due to the fact that the sensors were originally designed to monitor the movement of aircraft in wind tunnels! Clearly there are high-flyers in education authorities as well as in classrooms.) Looking at it from a Waldorf perspective, one cannot help wondering if such a measure is not some kind of pendulum swing brought about through the neglect, or at least the non-realization, of what is surely staring us in the face: *the pre-dominant activity in the early years is in the limbs.*

Returning to the will of the young child, given the time, spatial and budgetary constraints of modern life, what can be done? Possibilities include restoring some older practices but in a modern way, e.g. setting nursery rhymes to new pen-tatonic melodies, since the old ones no longer play a central part in culture, and 'acting' them while singing. The so-called 'riddles' of traditional nursery rhymes (e.g. Jack and Jill, Humpty Dumpty, Ring a Ring o' Roses) are often linked with historic events. But more to the point of child development in the early years is what the carer has in the back of his mind as a creative interpretation of the riddles *while he sings*, this then becoming a stimulant for the kind of non-verbal teaching/learning which is conveyed via body language, tone of voice, etc. in the child's best interests.*

Other possibilities are: protecting from extremes of modern culture; where there's a viable choice, finding a child minder rather than bundle the children into the car to drive for an hour or more to the airport to meet the grandparents; resisting where possible cooking with cheap, processed foods, often the product of high yielding yet low nutrition value crops; avoiding leaving glossy mags on the coffee table; putting the less artistic Christmas card in your own study where you can appreciate the thought behind it; counter-acting some of the attacks on children's will via the senses which undermine the life forces (by providing beautifully coloured playthings, for instance), and taking a little extra time to prepare attractive meals; replacing comfortably passive acquired habits with more active ways, and so on. And I repeat: none of these options is a simple matter in modern life—indeed, in some cases something of a social-Everest climb.

I seem to have erred towards the style of an agony aunt's column. So let me conclude by lobbing the ball back into the reader's court with an innocent question. If, while you were quietly queue-chatting, you had become aware of the spectacle of a two-year-old shrieking, 'I'm allowed,' his will

---

* Dr Janine Spencer, a development psychologist at Brunel University, enthused over nursery rhymes' other educational benefits: 'commu-nication, memory, language skills...' in an interview with *The Times* recently (9 July 2007).

intoxicated with a treasure-hoard of unguarded hazel nuts just pleading to be released from their tub-bondage, how would you have reacted? Melancholically? Cholerically? Phlegmatically? Sanguinically? As the proprietress did? Or in some other way? At the same time you will probably resolve not to allow your weathered eyelid to droop with unawareness in future! It's all a matter of *will*.

24. Delegation and Collegiality

Senses and Sense-perception—The Basis of Judgement—
Quality of Music-making Instrument—Budgetary Priorities

'*. . . the last rites!*'
The audience barely squeezed into the tastefully furnished
room where we were scheduled to play—the family string
quartet with the addition of a friend from Scotland who
played viola in the Mozart quintet and in the Schumann
piano quintet. One of my tasks was to introduce the items.
There were usually three components to these introductions
(some reference to the audience, something about the per-
formers and a word about the composer and his music), the
emphasis depending on the audience. The important thing
was to provide a comfortable link between listeners and
music. Which man in the street, after all, has even heard of let
alone heard Mozart's two-viola quintets? Yet they are among
his finest works.

On this occasion, our hosts who had welcomed us on
arrival, and who had shown us round, had made a point of
the piano being a recent acquisition. In my opening introductory remarks I decided to make a big thing of this, the
'new piano': 'And to be the first ensemble to give a concert
using your brand new piano is a special pleasure and honour.'
I could hear myself in danger of going over the top, especially
as I realized that the brand-newness was relative. The
instrument, a modest upright, had undergone a major
overhaul between leaving the auction room and arriving at its
new destination. Moreover, I was not the only one with the
perception of going over the top. But while those in the

audience responsible for the purchase of the instrument sat there glowing at this apparent condoning of their choice—though I hadn't meant it that way, as we had had little time to rehearse beyond tuning up the string instruments and getting a feel for the acoustics, and I had consequently had to take the quality of the instrument on trust—there was one particularly outspoken, choleric member of staff who clearly felt otherwise. She was sitting somewhere at the back of the room and, unbeknown to me, was fuming. When, therefore, I finally capped it all with '. . . to have, in fact, the honour of *baptizing* your . . .' I got no further: the choleric's fuse had reached its end. 'More like, give it the last rites,' she snapped, in a tone of voice that was an indelicate mixture of barely subdued outrage, undisguised scorn and resigned disgruntlement!

The theme of how one supports colleagues who are delegated to a particular task when it turns out other than you had expected is a tricky one that I cannot dwell on here, particularly as I do not know whether the institution in question had proceeded in this manner of delegation. To do so would be a fairly common way—sensible, too—of dealing with such a situation in the kind of Waldorf school which worked with the principle of a College of Teachers, delegating certain tasks in the way Steiner indicated, tasks that manifestly do not directly involve everyone. The purchase of a piano clearly comes into this category. The mind boggles at the thought of a College of 20 or 30 members all turning up at an auction and bidding communally as the baffled auctioneer, with his poised gavel hovering ever higher in mid-air, reiterates *going, going, going . . . going . . .* until the College, lightningly contracted into a scrum of decision-making, arrives at the point of unanimity! So I will leave this theme on one side and escape with relief to that of the pedagogical issues related to *quality of instrument*!

★   ★   ★

I was surprised one Friday at the end of October 2005, when tuning in somewhat late on the BBC radio's *Today* programme in order to get the news, to hear a professor of recorder at one of the London music colleges playing a piece by Bach. Was I on the right wavelength? A movement for unaccompanied baroque treble recorder composed by Johann Sebastian Bach, no less, at 0830 in the morning sounded odd, to say the least. And it was thrust, with hardly a semicolon to allow the mind to adjust, right next to the new Iranian president's outburst about wiping the State of Israel off the map and the barrage of diplomatic condemnation that thundered from across the spectrum of the United Nations, which the media were seemingly relishing sending out over the air umpteen times. Notwithstanding, I listened further. The professor was commenting on the quality of tone that a cheap plastic recorder is capable of compared with the beautifully tuned—and exquisitely played—instrument that he was using. Murmurs of genuine approval from the presenters followed: 'I never knew a recorder could sound like that.' The 'story' it transpired was about the 'cacophony', as the professor put it, produced by a large classful of small children blowing at different pressures through cheap plastic, with varying degrees of finger dexterity, it goes without saying—and, of course, the pain-in-the-neck (not to mention the ear) mischief-maker who has discovered that by keeping a straight face so as to be undetectable while simultaneously tensing the diaphragm and thereby sending an unrestrained burst of breath through the mouthpiece he can make a shrieking noise which raises to the nth degree the excruciating quality of the sound produced by his hit-and-miss peers in the chorus.

A dilemma for any educational set-up. When the governmental allocation—or, in the case of most Waldorf schools, the parental purse—is limited, how do you do justice to the acute sensitivity of young children, precisely in the early years when their sense impressions are at their most impressionable and go deepest psychologically as well as physiologically, and will form the basis for various kinds of judgement in later life? The Victorian adage was reputedly 'Spare the rod, spoil the child'. Today, it could read 'Deny the cash, ruin the senses'! We respect the physical body as far as identifiably detectable corporal punishment is concerned, but seldom get far with our respect for the finer sentiments rooted in soul and spirit, let alone with our understanding of the kind of subtlety that Steiner described whereby the physical body itself, *right into the inner organs*, is affected by the impressions children receive through their *unrestrained, utterly trusting reception of the world* via the wide open gateways of their young, developing senses.

Providing quality instruments for children to play on, especially in the early years when the senses are at their highest point of reception, is not necessarily the result of the financial constraints to which we are subjected. The same, of course, goes for the quality of coloured crayons or paints, furniture, food, clothing, exposing the children to inferior art on the walls, to shoddy building or unnatural materials from which their toys are made, or (to risk treading on very personal ground) a quality of voice inappropriate to the young child. In most cases, undoubtedly, yes. In most cases, I suspect, it is more a matter of adult thinking that is closer to the 'last rites'—not the sacramental aspect!—than to the creative future that we associate with the baptismal end of life. For example, money not spent on a few cinema tickets would go a long way towards paying for a well-manufactured recorder—the difference, say, between its cost and that of the cheap plastic model that the professor on the radio was decrying. It all depends on to 'which' expenditure column you assign 'what'. Is the expensive box of coloured crayons the luxury and the drive down to the coast (CO_2 emissions notwithstanding) a standard budget item, or vice versa? By definition, young families are at their most vulnerable when it comes to income and expenditure.

But this is getting close to sacrosanct ground and I feel uncomfortable lest I tread on it. However, when it comes to giving the senses of one's child a healthy foundation for life— sight, hearing, taste, touch and smell, as well as all those other senses which Steiner identified as vital in a child's schooling— it is worth reassessing the situation, not only at school, but also concerning the quality of home life. The reassessment might have a healthy impact all round. Be that as it may, the last rites for the senses, connected with brain and other aspects of development as they are, are surely the last thing that education should be celebrating.

25. Educational Terrorism?

A Government Curriculum for Under-Fives—College
Consensus—Nanny State—Unconscious Learning—Play—
Imitation and Authority—Mechanization—Staff
Appointments—Exam Preparation—Ego

'Yes, I accept him.'
The outcry from the British public on the dreary November
day 2005 following the announcement of the Government's
legislative plans to bring in a 'curriculum' for under-fives
took up an immense amount of media space, filling up
column after column even in the face of the House of
Commons seething over the Anti-Terrorism Bill concerning
which the division saw two senior ministers flown back from
missions abroad (Russia and Israel) to cast their vote, and
against which no fewer than eleven MPs who had held
previous ministerial positions rebelled against their own
Government, causing the Prime Minister's first defeat in his
long term of office. I was waiting for the final thunderclap to
burst and for someone to point out that legal insistence on
such formal early learning was tantamount to an act of *educational terrorism* against which babies and toddlers need protection. This seemed particularly poignant as the Pisa research
of 2003, still living boldly in the memory, had shown that the
best education in the world was to be found in Finland and a
key factor was that formal learning did not take place before
the seventh year.

One columnist, though as far as I know unaware of
Steiner's leading thoughts concerning the basis for education
in the first seven years, pinpointed exactly what happens after

the birth of a child and therefore what she felt should be left free to *happen naturally*. It was Miriam Stoppard in the *Daily Telegraph* who, in elaborating certain aspects of child development, drew attention to the 'mastering [of] the most difficult skills it will ever have to acquire, in the form of walking, and speaking'. She was coming from the direction of brain development and, in referring to the tripling of the brain (i.e. its weight) in the first year of life, held that we cannot 'hope to anticipate exactly how a baby's brain will soak up experience and learn'. She went on to make the case for allowing babies to *develop in their own time*, unforced, in an 'informal, deconstructed, environment' when the baby has 'free rein' and (above all) thus should learn 'unconsciously'.

★ ★ ★

Steiner did venture at least to point in the direction of anticipating exactly how a baby learns: it is by means of *imitation*. The exactness of the imitative forces could also be gone into with a toothcomb, of course. But the overall axiom can be encapsulated in that one word. At the entrance of Dante's Inferno stands the awe-inspiring warning to the unwary: All who enter here must abandon hope (*Lasciate omni speranza voi che entratequi*). Invisibly inscribed over every nursery door—be it in the home or an organized nursery—could well be a motto extolling the baby's inborn power of imitation as that which provides the adult with the key to its development and therefore to hope in the future. In an environment where the adult stands upright and walks, the baby 'learns' to walk. In an environment where the adults talk to one another and to the baby, the baby 'learns' to speak a human language—this we happily call the *mother tongue*.

From the moment a child enters a Steiner Kindergarten, Nursery or Playgroup—are those ministers listening?

*Play*group—the world of imitation comes into full expression. The Kindergarten teacher may be podding broad beans as the children arrive first thing in the morning. Not all of them will want to join in; many will have their own drives to play out: previous experiences at home, or on the bus journey to school, or at the market, or from visiting a relative or friend ... experiences which provided an appetite for the hungry-to-imitate memory. In favourite corners of the room or freely 'contained' areas which they create (by spreading out cushions, maybe) you will see, second-hand, as it were, the apple-seller, the dentist, the mother taking clothes out of the washing machine, the bus driver, the post lady with her bag of letters, the priest conducting a baptism (a ceremony that is becoming increasingly popular in our non-marital social climate). In earlier days it would have been the road sweeper, the milkman delivering white clanky bottles of milk onto the back doorstep, the ploughman turning the stubble fields into earth-rich furrows, the butcher in his boater and long blue and white stripy apron, and so on. Striding backwards, century by century, life itself without any trimmings was an Aladdin's cave of treasures for the young child's forces of imitation; mechanization has opened the gateway to much adult freedom but usurped imitation from where it had reigned since time immemorial on the throne of childhood.

Economic pressures are often so great nowadays that families are reduced to time-saving devices to get them through the day, and costly leisure activities on Saturdays and Sundays to get them through the week. But where there is a choice (such as baking the occasional cake instead of stockpiling the freezer, or sailing or going for a family walk, say, instead of swelling the ranks of the yelling crowd at a soccer match), it can make all the difference to that part of children's development—a huge part—in which their capacity for imitation is acknowledged in some way. Ironically, it is becoming easier to cater for this in the Kindergarten than in the modern home environment, for a hands-on ambience can be professionally cultivated there, which would look oddly anachronistic in the home and might feel at first somewhat retrogressive.

We don't, of course, relapse into the early stages of arithmetic if we need to check the telephone bill—counting out aloud and using our fingers to add up! We probably even take it on trust, despite trust being a quality less and less taken for granted, and increasingly outlawed or marginalized by the nanny state—whose nannying involves less nurturing and the professional equivalent of TLC (tender loving care), and whose nanny's aprons more and more resemble barristers' wigs and police riot gear. However, a mental activity such as arithmetic is in a very different category from mechanized transport, industrially generated forms of cooking, the power tools we use for hedge-cutting, shaving or even screwdriving a screw into a piece of wood.

Faced with the challenge—for such it is—that a young child's basic asset is imitation and that it is the adult's example of *will* manifested in manual work, hands-on activity, etc., in which the asset can be invested, we understandably shrink back, protesting perhaps that you can't put the clock back. Subscribing, however, to the rampant inflation of mechanized life, notionally to save time and effort, will assuredly leave the child's greatest asset uninvested. The benefit from a healthy imitative childhood, particularly in the first seven years, will dwindle and the future adult will be left to pay the price—the negative equity of an imitatively-endowed will that has been ignored or, worse, subject to a statutory enforced curriculum that trespasses even on the virgin ground of 'learning' to walk and talk and, of course, thereby *think*—

that vital third stage of human development which the *Telegraph* columnist implied but didn't have column space to spell out.

★   ★   ★

In a Steiner school, which follows the advice Steiner gave about staffing, employment decisions are made by those whose karma it will be to work with the new colleague *as a full team*. These are amongst the profoundest levels of working with the will—*reaching a consensus*—that can then be put into practical life. The body undertaking this corporate life responsibility is often referred to as the *College of Teachers*.

During each year there is always one decision to be made which concerns the appointment of the new Class 1 teacher. Other teachers will come and go, of course, but one cannot anticipate such changes to the same extent, e.g. when the metalwork teacher might move on, or (sadly unavoidable from time to time) when a teacher may have to retire on the grounds of poor health. Each September, on the other hand (New Year usually in the Southern Hemisphere), children 'come up' from the Kindergarten into the Lower School to start the journey from Class 1 to Class 12—and in some cases, Class 13, where the school follows the example of the first Waldorf School, where the Waldorf element which imbued the entire education was completed at the end of Class 12 and the thirteenth class was added for the purposes of '*exam preparation*' as Steiner referred to it. (There are other approaches to the problem of equipping pupils externally so that they can get their entrance ticket (exam qualifications) to the next stage of life—apprenticeships, higher education, etc.—without encroaching too much on, and therefore compromising, the Waldorf approach.)

Thus entry into Class 1 is perhaps the greatest educational

threshold that a child can cross. The watchword for the teacher also changes at this stage from *imitation to authority*.

In imitation the children are completely given up to that which they are imitating. I use the *passive* voice 'are given up to' advisedly. In order to give yourself up to something (i.e. the *active* form), there has to be a conscious 'you' there in the first place, an ego. At the level of bodily function, that which digests the almond—when the drive of hunger leads us to eat one—remains in the unconscious. The starting point of imitation is similar—but at the soul-spirit level, notwithstanding its bodily effect, as when the child is 'learning' to speak with all its myriad neural implications.

As the incarnation of the child proceeds, however, it engenders *self*-awareness. The long journey from unconsciousness to consciousness (even, perhaps, through lifelong development to super-consciousness) takes place. The first moment of incisively saying 'I' (usually, but not always, in the third year) and the Rubicon stage of development at the 9th/10th year (Steiner indicates a fairly broad band of possibility) are the first two major milestones on this journey. They are not coincidental with the septennial phases of childhood to which the Waldorf approach to education pays heed. It is as if the seven-year rhythm moves from the past—from birth—through life, continuing into adulthood: 21, 28, 35, 42, etc., whilst the ego, with a different and less defined rhythm, shines in from the future. While there is a *certainty* about the rhythm of seven, there is an air not of uncertainty but of *freedom* about the ego. It can be seen, after all, in its full development as the goal of evolution!

Thus, increasing the ego-consciousness in the second period of childhood, from 7 to 14, calls for the teacher to change her stance from being the one whose deeds (and what motivated them) are worthy of the child's imitative forces to one whose manner inspires the child to choose to follow her as an *authority*.

The shift is subtle but precise and often has repercussions in the parent's perception of the teacher. Entering a Waldorf Kindergarten, parents frequently warm to the atmosphere, identify with it immediately and heave a sigh of relief that they have found what they want for their child. Other details follow. Entering a Waldorf school and realizing your child will be taught main-lessons by the same teacher for eight years (though the law prevents this ideal in Holland and some other places) poses other questions, questions which can boil down to 'Is he or she likely to be the authority who will inspire my child's learning and nurture my child's develop-ment?' The same equally applies to the teacher of French, movement, handwork, or other so-called subject lessons, of course.

★ ★ ★

It was when a College of Teachers was duly considering the appointment of a new colleague for the next Class 1 that, after considering the short-listed applicants in a meeting of the College, an unusually long and not entirely comfortable period of discussion ensued in order to reach consensus. What Steiner refers to as 'karmic-instinct' clearly came into play. The chairperson eventually asked each member to affirm that they agreed with her sense that *consensus* had arrived, and pointed towards a particular candidate. Each person responded as they 'went round the table' but when it came to a particularly choleric member of the College, whose standards of authority continued well into her Upper School science lessons (with robust and excellent results!), instead of simply responding 'Yes', like her colleagues, she gave a hint of what she had been going through inwardly and possibly the reservations she had been wrestling with to arrive at consent, her son being in the class. There was an intense pause of four or five seconds, followed by what seemed like an arrow speeding from the bow as she flung out: 'Yes, I *accept* him!'

THE WIDER VISION
(WELTMENSCH)

26. Individual and Collegial Group

College of Teachers—Decision Making—Delegation—
Wonder—Initiative—Teacher Education—Science
Teaching—Goethean Phenomenology

'You look terribly worried.'
It was Steiner's firm contention that the College of Teachers'
meeting was the place where *teacher education* (though the
expression has only crept into circulation recently) rightly
happened. To begin with, when the Waldorf School in
Stuttgart first opened its doors, the College of Teachers was a
small group and all teachers belonged to it, irrespective of the
age group they were teaching. Intellectual superiority played
no part in Waldorf. College meetings were where pedagogical questions were discussed, where the understanding of
childhood generally was furthered, where the situation of
pupils in the school was reported and discussed, where
practicalities such as what emphasis to give to this or that
subject on the timetable were sorted out, where the curriculum—especially that for the upper classes as they were
'added' year by year—was mooted, outlined, evolved (based
on Steiner's suggestions, of course), its rationale gone into,
and so on.

When the stone carver stands before his monolith of
marble, mallet and chisel in hand, the lengthy process of
moving from design (his evolving idea) to placing the finished
statue on its plinth *begins its course*. However fast the stone
chips may fly left and right, the process is a slow one as each
turn of the chisel-guiding wrist and each resounding blow
with the mallet nudges that which is supersensible (i.e.

existing only in the sculptor's mind) towards becoming an object of solid, marbled sense-perception. So it was with Steiner education as it strove to nudge its way into Waldorf praxis and continues to do so, year in, year out. From this point of view, to present them as synonymous (as might easily be assumed with terms such as *Steiner Waldorf*) borders on the deceiving.

Where it was a matter of school policy being established, Steiner gave clear indications of what was going on spiritually for a group of individuals—and how eminently talented they were—to work not only as a 'research cluster' which shares insights and engages in discussion but which also reaches consensual *decisions*, by being open to higher guidance in the process, i.e. more than would normally be accessible to a single individual. Of course, there had to be some *delegation*, as Steiner called it, once the general direction/destination had been decided upon. But staffing was one of certain matters which were vital to the school's well-being; he was adamant that appointments should be made only with the highest guidance available, and that meant involvement of the whole group working their way through to consensus.

In time (not very much time), the school grew to such wall-bursting proportions that the teaching body became too large for such a non-hierarchical way of working with all school business. Not only that, some teachers who were excellent at their work in the classroom—the *raison d'être* for being at the school—did not necessarily want to carry combined responsibility for the school as a whole. This is still the case today in the majority of Waldorf schools. Hence teacher education takes place in meetings to which all teachers attend with the frequent result of shortening College agenda. To what extent this might impact upon the way Waldorf edges its way towards Steiner we may leave on one side here.

In all the complexity of organizing meetings, however, and determining which item is placed on which agenda, it is imperative to keep the classroom in sight. It is there that the teacher's full, individual *initiative*—and how Steiner emphasized the central necessity of this—comes to expression. In every moment of every lesson the teacher's initiative stands on its own, yields its abundant harvest, albeit tuned to school policy on the one hand, as the violinist's instrument is in tune with the rest of the orchestra and, on the other hand, tuned wherever possible to an anthroposophical world view. Her presentation, her classroom discipline, her interaction with pupils, her on-the-spot insights into subject matter or into methods of teaching it all depend on initiative. The flow of initiative can always be strengthened by the teacher education sessions that go on in Teachers' or College meetings, but the initiative itself is a matter of personal drive, entirely individual—with, of course, all the imagination, inspiration and intuition that the individuality can muster. And so in the organization of a Waldorf school working along the lines that Steiner set out as a matter of professional 'discipline' the individual's domain (self-evidently) is the classroom, whereas the 'boardroom' (or whatever it is called) is the domain where individuals work as a group with very clear procedures that incorporate the spiritual potential of colleagues sharing the same aims and inspired by the same philosophy of education.

To return to our sculptor's atelier, chisel and mallet function together. Without the mallet the chisel would do little more than scratch the surface of the marble ineffectually. Without the chisel the mallet would do little more than bludgeon. In neither case would the design appear in all its aesthetic beauty. In the meetings Steiner had with the Waldorf teachers—there were some 70 of them officially recorded—we meet an archetypal situation. Steiner's many portrayals of what education could accomplish needed to develop into Waldorf praxis—again, through the initiative of teachers. And in the ferment of a new beginning, in reading about the chiselling process—which is available to us in the published *Konferenzen* as they were called in German—we can get some idea of how the marble chips flew fast and furious, during the course of an enormously generous five years, in which time both 'theory' and praxis evolved. It would, of course, be a gross error to imagine that they fused instantly. In fact we still struggle with the fusion. The struggle, moreover, is likely to have unfortunate, even devastating, side effects *if we confuse the process of decision making through Collegial consensus with how one individual comes to a decision* (irrespective of whether or not that individual has 'consulted' with others).

★   ★   ★

In the early 60s I had taken over a class during their last three years of the Lower School from a teacher who went to America. The task was nothing if not challenging: in Class 6 bringing the history up to the end of the Middle Ages, taking the first steps in Euclidean geometry, the exciting prospect of Europe lying at your geographical feet just waiting to be 'discovered', opening the gateway into the whole field of science, to mention only some of the curriculum. Colleagues were very supportive. Fellow class teachers gave valuable time to preview the main-lessons, and I regularly met up with one particular colleague, who *hosted* my arrival on the teaching body of the school. The notion of 'mentors' had not, at that time, begun to shift the centre of gravity of teacher education away from the College of Teachers' meetings.

But even a cursory glance at the ground to be covered will convince anyone that it is unlikely that everything the class teacher of 12-, 13- and 14-year-olds has to accomplish is likely to be at the beck and call of the average person before they set out on the lengthy and, at times, demanding journey.

On the occasion in question we had travelled as far as Class 8 and the second science main-lesson of the year. In Waldorf circles there are essentially two schools of thought regarding Lower School science education in physics, though it could be argued that they both amount to the same thing—to give the pupils a basic grounding in the seven branches of physics: sound, light, colour, heat, magnetism, electricity and mechanics. These are all taken further, of course, and other branches of knowledge are added to them in the Upper School. The two schools of thought apply to the first six branches, mechanics being a main-lesson in its own right and normally taught in Class 7. One school of thought advocates spreading the six topics evenly over the three years: sound and light in Class 6 (or, as an alternative, sound and colour, since colour offers more artistic application of science than does light), colour (or light) and heat in Class 7, and magnetism and electricity in Class 8. The other school of thought covers all six topics in each of the three years, each year building on work done previously (naturally with a corresponding adjustment of the time allowed to each).

On my first round with Classes 6, 7 and 8 I adopted the second school of thought. For one thing, it had the practical advantage of being more bite size. My last 'serious' pursuit of science had been a module of acoustics, taken as part of my first university degree, and, before that, GCSE physics—all of it as I write every bit of 60 cobwebby years ago! However, though influenced by the need to scrape the rust off my scientific knowledge—as is the case with many whose life's course brings them to class teaching—what convinced me to take the same route eight years later (and again with my third cohort of pupils) was the way the division of subjects seemed to accommodate itself so harmoniously to the developmental process through which the young teenager is going during these three years, the transition from childhood to youth.

This means that in Class 6 one can concentrate as much as possible on *natural* phenomena: sounds heard in the natural environment; the diurnal/nocturnal occurrence of light and darkness, and the play of light in reflection, refraction and similar phenomena; the wealth of colour phenomena in the skies and in simple everyday experiences; the effects of heat and cold in nature's crucible and in ordinary human life; and the most elementary manifestations of magnetism and static electricity. All these phenomena can be experienced either in the natural world or with the help of very familiar household objects.

Because the 'awakening' process at the dawn of causal phenomenological thinking is close to home, I believe, there is therefore a chance that the *sense of wonder* during the pursuit of knowledge, will be retained and will echo on from the child's earlier, starry-eyed years. The accumulating wonder-wed knowledge then leads to a spirit of enquiry, a fact strongly underpinned by the so-called *Goethean approach to science*, which cultivates both a hunger for the 'wisdom' concealed in the outer phenomena and a development of the kind of thinking which seeks to explain it.

Building on the above, in the seventh class many of the phenomena of the six branches of science encountered in Class 6 are revisited, now with the help of experimental equipment brought into the classroom to simulate, isolate and make more apparent what otherwise occurs in nature. Thereafter, as the ongoing study gets more scientifically sophisticated, it usually becomes necessary to move into the physics lab and use apparatus hitherto unfamiliar, taking us into Class 8.

★　★　★

It is probably because of such considerations that the Dutch Government ruled, some years back (and the Belgians have followed suit), that teachers of secondary school age should have degrees in the subjects they teach. One can understand this argument, though from a Waldorf pedagogical point of view certainly not sympathize with it. Notwithstanding, there are moments, particularly in Class 8, when you feel, as a class teacher, one more fathom and you would be out of your depth. Even if you have practised an experiment *successfully(!)* the evening before as part of your preparation, there can remain an element of the performing artist's nervousness when, with a couple of dozen pairs of eyes watching both the experiment *and you*, you connect the final terminal, or—in chemistry experiments, notorious for not being as 'reliable' as those in physics—with sometimes feigned aplomb you tap the 'magic' powder so that it trickles from the test tube into the retort in which the desired reaction is going to occur, imprinting itself (hopefully not explosively) on the senses and on the memory of your pupils for all time.

It was precisely on such an occasion, in the physics lab, that one of the pupils broke the silence that hung in the air of anticipation a split second before the scientific critical moment. Studying the expression on my face, she blurted out: 'Mr Masters, you look terribly worried.' If you'd asked me 40 years ago what the experiment was, I would have remembered clearly. Now, almost everything except the half-quizzical, half-amused, half-accusing, half-impish look on her face as I glanced up at where she was sitting in the front row of the demonstration lab, and the bull's-eye she succeeded in shooting with those six words, has been forgotten. However, be it known, she took up teaching as a career and rose high in her chosen profession, though regretfully I do not have any information regarding the degree of virtuosity, if any, she was wont to demonstrate whilst performing tricky experiments (or experimental tricks, for that matter) which involved tinkering with 240 volts in the physics lab!

Creditable though programmes are, such as the trip to the Nasa space centre in Cape Canaveral (Florida) set up by the International Space Station Educational Trust (ISSET) or the site of the Apollo I tragedy where three astronauts met their death in fire on a space test, they cannot be the general educational answer to the declining interest in science in schools. When Rosamund Franklin, the DNA pioneer, was asked a few years ago why she gave up pure science for popular science in the media she pointed to the *method* of teaching—too focused and too narrow. It is surely predictable that a method that consists of following a set of instructions which the student in the lab has to follow rigidly to attain a predetermined result (a so-called *experiment*?!) is not going to touch the child-inherited sense of wonder on which Goethean phenomenology depends.

27. What Happened to the European Conventions and Declarations to Which the UK was Signatory?

Between the Devil of Non-affordability and the Deep Blue Sea of Compromise—Educational Philosophy— 'Choice' by Lottery

'Minister, you say you support us: How?'

It was a meeting in the House of Commons, some 20 years ago. It followed in the footsteps—giant footsteps across the decades—of similar occasions with the Government of the day. These had been instigated by eminent people in the Waldorf Movement such as A.C. Harwood in the post-war years and R.A. Jarman, a previous chairman of the Steiner Schools Fellowship, the charity which, among other aims and responsibilities, represented the schools at national level. On this occasion the deputation consisted of officers from the Fellowship, parents and teachers, and was thought to be representative. On the other side of the table sat Sir Keith Joseph, Secretary of State, and senior civil servants from the Education Department.

There were two points at issue, both connected and essentially political, though having educational implications in one case and economic in the other.

(i) The European Convention for the Protection of Human Rights and Fundamental Freedoms (20 March 1952) states that the State shall 'ensure' the *right of parents to choose* the type of education they want for

their child in conformity with their own ... philosophical convictions.

(ii) With reference to the same declaration was the plea that
surely if the taxpayer's money is used for funding education (hitherto limited essentially to *mainstream* provision) it is his/her right to receive an equal amount of
funding (per capita or in whatever way the State deems
fair) for the choice the parent(s) freely make—this being
the conclusion gleaned from further declarations made in
the European Parliament in 1984, 1989 (Vienna) and
1991 (Helsinki), for details of which see the collation
published by Prof. Siegfried Jenkner of the European
Forum for Freedom in Education in 1992—ISBN
3-924391-09-2.

The Government at the time of the said meeting was
experienced as iron-hard right wing. Not that being left of
centre necessarily makes officialdom immune from party-
driven obstinacy. There was the painful case in June this year
(2007) when the General Teaching Council (GTC) and
other high-profile bodies voiced one of its weightiest con-
demnations yet of school testing (in the form of SATS). It is
therefore not surprising that it was some years before our
lobbying got Steiner education onto the agenda of a formal
Committee. The breakthrough occasion was when the
Labour spokesperson stated that his Party had become convinced that the Steiner schools in the country (in effect
England and Wales) were not elitist and that if Labour got
into power it would support them. This, for the record, was
due to a large extent to the educational insight of Cynog
Dafis, MP at the time for the Welsh National Party (Plaid
Cymru), who had been impressed when visiting the Nant-y-
Cwm Steiner school, where pretty well all the parents had

written letters, lobbying for the recognition of the Waldorf schools. Mr Dafis then followed through his conviction that the education had something vital to offer by getting the political wheels oiled more than had ever happened before. The rest is history and can be read up in *Hansard* and in archives elsewhere.

On the occasion in question, we were not so advanced. I suppose one could hardly have expected government funding in a political arena that supported the 'upwardly mobile' to the hilt and appeared ruthlessly content (not only to the protesting Opposition parties who had an eye on social issues) to let the 'devil take the hindmost'.

One could appreciate the Government's problems. It had two hot potatoes:

(i)   If we support Waldorf schools and permit them to move from the Independent Sector to the State Sector we will also have to support *faith schools*, which are similarly hammering on the door;

(ii) If we support Waldorf parents and give them money to 'ensure' their educational choice, we will be obliged to do the same for parents who choose public schools [in the UK these are private and attract very high tuition fees] for their children.

The first, though it was never said in so many words, implied reluctance to acknowledge the rights of those swathes of the population with religious views other than so-called Christian, a reluctance that has since begun to yield slightly. The second clearly suggested considerable budgetary implications. The Government thus hedged its bets. It shouted ever louder and clearer that it was standing for parents' rights by giving them the opportunity to choose *which school*—completely pulling the wool over many people's eyes by avoiding pointing out that the point at issue was not 'which school' but *which education*. The recent pendulum swing to 'choice' of school by lottery, which has created such a backlash in Brighton (February/March 2007) in a last-straw kind of attempt to put a veneer of democracy on this issue of parental choice, ignores the European Convention which supports parents' *philosophical* convictions.

★ ★ ★

With reference to the meeting in question, the stonewalling of the establishment did present a minute chink of light at one point when a cross-party group of socially minded peers set up the Committee for Educational Choice, the three main parties being represented by excellent people in their various fields: Baroness Cox, a real fighter for the under-privileged both at home and abroad, Lord Grimmond, prominent in higher education, and Lord Young of Dartington, founder of the Open University. It also so happened that the last of these, Lord Young, was aware of Steiner's philosophy; indeed, the translation into English of the biography of his grandfather, D.N. Dunlop, founder of the World Power Conference was about to come off the press— Dunlop was held in the highest esteem by Rudolf Steiner.

The meetings called by the Committee made a little headway, but it was clear that there were gaps that would have to be closed politically before the country would put the international declarations and conventions to which it had been signatory into real practice, as Denmark had done. Moreover, there were gulfs beyond imagination before the country would even contemplate a measure such as exists now in the Czech Republic where schools—of whatever educational philosophy—are not allowed registration *unless* 'founded' and funded by the State. It did not, of course, make matters easier that at the time we were insisting on the kind of freedom vis-à-vis the *education as such* that Steiner had envisaged—this being reflected in the name of the first school, the Free Waldorf School (*Freie Waldorfschule*), i.e. liberal, not *gratis!*

The 'strings-attached' problems in State-funded Waldorf education experienced in various countries across the world shifts the conflict away from the financial sacrifice of *parent* (who pays in effect twice over, once through tax and once through any financial contribution or school fee) and *teacher* (whose salary suffers unduly in order to keep unavoidable fees/contributions as low as possible for the sake of those parents in low income brackets whose philosophical convictions prompt them to choose Steiner education). However, the conflict doesn't go away, but gains entry to the *child's* experience in the classroom—that is, whenever genuine Waldorf becomes compromised in one way or another through the one who pays the piper stipulating what educational tune the piper shall play.

The above, without dotting all the i's and crossing all the t's, gives some idea of the issues raised during the discussion on the occasion in question. Indeed, at root there is no other issue that is relevant to the rights of all concerned, however much one tries to disguise the fact.

As time allotted to the meeting was running out and it became apparent that the stern front put up by Secretary of State and bureaucrats was likely to remain unyielding, a parent (a factory owner in an industrial part of the country) spoke up for the first time and fairly heatedly challenged: 'Minister, you say you support us: *How?*' The reply came without hesitation, not quite in a snarling tone of voice but certainly aloof and grim: 'By letting you exist!'—which was more than Stalin or Hitler had permitted. But it was hardly in line with the Declaration of Human Rights, the text of which had fanned our hopes and motivation.

A blessing in disguise? Not if you are a parent or teacher looking into your unreplenished wallet, of course. But for the blossoming of the education without any *outside* encroachments, there were indisputable advantages. There is a toy (variously named according to the manufacturer) consisting of a wooden manikin that goes clump clump from one side to the other as it 'walks' down a gentle incline. Let us not lay undue stress on the fact that it can only go *down*! More pertinent here is what Steiner saw as the need to be clear about the respective tasks of the *political* and *cultural* spheres of society. The former should be concerned pre-eminently with—and *only* with—human rights. Education, which he placed in the cultural sphere, should not be interfered with by the State either in theory or praxis, or whether it is clumping left or right. Where these spheres have become confused, experience across the world shows that *educational progress* is almost without exception hampered.

Thankfulness, therefore, to be 'allowed to exist', but Minister, what about those *rights*?

28. Who You Meet is What Counts

Education Authorities—Action Stations—Official Visits
to Israel

'If he were a woman . . .'
Of all the unlikely contexts, it was during the Gulf War.
Though things were hotting up between Iraq and Israel,
colleagues over there apparently had no reason to cancel the
long-planned visit. This was despite the fear that Iraq had the
possibility of chemical warheads on its long-distance
weapons, a fear that proved to be more political speculation
than hard fact when finally the tension between the Bush
administration and Iraq snapped and the costly attack on
Baghdad was launched some years later—a can of worms
taking an inordinately long time to open.

Political speculation (or whatever is the correct term),
however, has dire consequences when the misinformation
coming 'from the top' is disseminated powerfully enough to
strike fear in the soul. Planes in and out of Tel Aviv were
cancelled (my flight was the last to land from London). All
schools were closed, and many other aspects of life ground to
a halt. People either sealed a room in their houses against
poisoned air or made for the nearest bunker, with ears glued
to the radio for almost continuous news bulletins.

It had its comic side, too. On the kibbutz where I was
staying, extra round-the-clock surveillance was put in place,
with the local Israelis—well trained through their annual
dose of conscription—manning their guard posts with
machine guns at the ready lest there be uprising from Arabs in
the neighbourhood. The comedy was the relaxed way in

which the 'territorials' dressed. There was no sign of anything approaching military uniform. One 'soldier' was even seen in a hand-made purple smock!

My colleagues back home, at that time very supportive of the work in which I was engaged on behalf of Steiner education, generously funded the extra cost of a flight to enable me to leave the country as soon as El Al (the first airline to 'brave it') opened the airport at Tel Aviv. On the way there we drove past the American cruise missiles deployed prominently beside the motorway against the dreaded Scuds. Security at the airport, always a lengthy process when leaving Israel, had reached gigantic proportions. The interrogation of passengers conducted by military security officers made the two or three questions asked routinely today at check-in, in the wake of recent terrorist attacks, seem like dwarfs beside Gog and Magog.

However, before I 'escaped'—I do not wish to exaggerate, though on the same night as my departure, the kibbutz bakery suffered damage from an Iraqi missile—there was work to be done. This could not be my usual visiting of classes in the Waldorf school, attending teachers' meetings, lecturing on the teacher training seminar and acting as advisor. The Waldorf school there is State funded, a very advantageous status gained through political lobbying at its inception. But even had that not been the case, and the school was not obliged to abide by certain State regulations (*not* affecting the pedagogy), no parent would have allowed their child out of the protection of the home (or bunker), the life-threatening state of tension being what it was. No, the work was with the authorities.

★   ★   ★

Two meetings had been scheduled, one locally and the other with the education department in Jerusalem, both of them to do with the ongoing 'recognition' of the school—and, of course, the battle for zero or, at most, minimum interference with curriculum and methodology. This is inevitable, regrettably but understandably, where public money is involved.

The first of these meetings happened virtually on my arrival. Still gaining my breath from the journey, I was more or less greeted with, 'Go and put a tie on, Brien; we want you to look English!' The kibbutz is situated in an otherwise Arab district with three presences: it is very close to a Bedouin settlement; an Arab village is situated within a mile; and one of the largest Arab towns in the land is less than ten minutes drive away. At the invitation of the Bedouins an official meeting had been arranged on their premises with inspectors from the local education authority. These being Arab, and the Iraqi attack on Israel imminent, the Israeli colleagues had assumed that the meeting would be cancelled. But to their surprise it was 'business as usual'.

I personally don't feel that the Englishman wearing his tie played a great part in the meeting, and in any case he didn't speak a word of either language. Perhaps his role was something of a smoke-detector, passively waiting to set alarm bells ringing if and when smoke appeared!? But it didn't. With the ambience exuded by the contagious good nature of the teacher who had been selected to represent the school (himself a high-ranking officer in the Israeli Army!), the lengthy and relaxed affair—the Bedouins plying us with delicious home-made pitta bread, hummus and dozens of other 'dips'—seemed to pass completely oblivious of the dangerous political situation. And this was despite the fact that my Israeli colleague at one point was totally up front with: 'And what do you think of what Saddam is doing?'

Bold of him, I remember thinking, but how wise to offer a psychological safety valve, so to speak.

The second meeting, in Jerusalem, was put on hold until it was deemed safe for people to move about more freely, the safety being attributed as much to the delivery and deployment of the American cruise missiles as to any second thought that Saddam might be having about his precipitous and provocative action. In both cases, the agenda is hardly worth mentioning here: more or less ongoing bureaucratic communication, but sufficiently beyond routine to warrant a 'Senior Academic Consultant' (part of the title conferred on me at the time) being in attendance.

Over the years, when I formally visited the Waldorf Movement in Israel (from 1987 onwards) there were several such meetings. This one remains outstanding in my memory because of the backdrop of war, naturally; but it is not the most memorable of all. The department of education in Jerusalem could hardly be less of a contrast with Whitehall, even if it tried. There are certainly no 'collars and ties' to be seen! The occasion I have in mind, therefore, was the most congenial official meeting ever. The minister, wearing his *kippa*, had paid an official visit to the Waldorf School in the Galilee area, situated on the kibbutz campus, and had gone into all classes. He had himself been a teacher. (Not all officials know all that much about the classroom!—an irony that has sadly found its reflection in other government departments, but which can be particularly devastating in education.)

Although the agenda was reasonably routine, it was lengthy and we went from point to point in a fairly informal yet efficient way. However, it was only at the end of the meeting, when the agenda had been exhausted, that all vestige of formality was thrown to the winds. While we sat there with eyebrows raised, the minister reminisced over his visit to the school. It was still small at that time but he was obviously enthusiastic about the teaching he had seen, the children's responsive attitude and their work. The climax came, however, when he was describing his visit to the class of the 'lead' teacher—lead in the sense of it being the class with the oldest age group in the school, the children having started in the Kindergarten. Their parents were amongst the initial pioneers, and were determined that Waldorf should be firmly placed on the Israeli educational map.

Although many of the teachers trained in England, this particular colleague (and his wife, a eurythmist) had received his initial training in Switzerland. Recalling the lesson in which he had been present, the minister's voice became more and more excited whilst his gestures grew more and more animated. Finally he paused, lost for superlatives and, not wishing to repeat himself any more, came up with the unforgettable comment: 'If that man were a woman and I had no wife, *I would marry him.*'

How unpredictable can you get? With this, although there were hurdles that had to be firmly stridden across in the years that followed, the establishment of Waldorf in Israel seemed as unassailable as anything could be expected to be in an uncertain, unpredictable-as-ministers, chemical-warheads-bee-lining-across-the-frontier kind of world.

29. The Adaptability of the Waldorf Curriculum

'Streams' in World History—Multi-ethnicity

'Getting quite Mexican.'
It was my introduction to the Spanish-speaking world. Somewhat surprisingly the contacts had come not through teachers but through two parents who were attending a course I was giving in Rudolf Steiner College, Sacramento. With searching eyes, strikingly beautiful Mexican features and beaming smiles they proposed a visit the following Easter. Though it was left 'up in the air' it was not long after their return home that colleagues from the Waldorf school in Cuernavaca contacted me with a firm invitation, and at its core was the question: 'What would the Waldorf curriculum be in *history* for a Mexican school?'

This touched a deep vein in me. In my researches into Henry the Navigator in the year which was the quater-centenary of his birth, I had obtained literature from the Portuguese Embassy in London which convinced me when I had to teach my first Class 7 history main-lesson in 1965 that, though Columbus is clearly a towering figure in the fifteenth-century story of the 'discoveries', at least equal emphasis should be given to the Portuguese side of the story. Not only did the commencement of Portugal's persistent and successful endeavour to round the South African Cape pre-date the Spanish conquest of the West, it seemed that despite its giant-size colony of Brazil the motivation behind the Portuguese explorations was very different in character from that of the Spaniards and was all rooted in what moved Portugal to strike out for independence from the Spanish throne in the first place. Added to this there were all the prelims (an inadequate expression considering the limelight they deserve) connected with the Portuguese capturing the Moors' harbour of Cueta, the harbour which commanded the Straits of Gibraltar from its strategic position on the north-western tip of Africa, prelims which are such excellent material for holding young adolescents enthralled in the intriguing transition from the chivalrous heritage of the Middle Ages to the dawn of what Steiner referred to as the age of the consciousness soul (the commencement of which he dates as 1413).

I suppose the bottom line has to be connected with the divergences that become apparent in the growth of Christianity. Portugal, led initially by Henry the Navigator, was deeply connected with the founding of the Order of Christ as a partial answer to the extermination of the Knights Templars. Spain—though it is difficult to avoid oversimplifying—promulgated a Christianity characterized by and dominated by the Inquisition. Be that as it may, it highlights the importance for the children to become acquainted with different 'streams' in history.

On a world scale, Steiner gave prominence in his anthroposophical lectures to the stream which 'travelled' from the Far East westwards, through what is now Iran, Iraq, Egypt, Greece, etc. He did not, however, undervalue the importance of other streams and there is no reason to assume that that was his intention in hardly ever referring to them. On the contrary, the fact that he recommends that lessons in geography (that most all-embracing of subjects) should include the *spiritual* geography of each place opens wide the door for meeting and valuing the ethnic background of each country, the religious beliefs of the indigenous populations (with sometimes layers to peel off) and their place in world evolution.

Quite rightly in view of this, the Waldorf colleagues in Mexico did not feel that the curriculum as fashioned in Stuttgart in 1919—far more loosely fashioned, incidentally, than is usually assumed to be the case—was something to be applied in Central America without further ado. That is to say, something as central to their own stream of history as the Mayan and Aztec civilizations needed more status than being a kind of adjunct to geography—whatever emphasis, spiritual or otherwise, might be given to the 'adjunct'. Hence the request, which was the external reason for my visit, to bring some objective thinking to bear (from someone who had no connection with Mexico, nor at that point in time with the Spanish- or Portuguese-speaking worlds).

On the one hand, I think it is fair to say I was well prepared for the task—three Class 7s in the class teaching part of my Waldorf career, and several lectures on the history curriculum in various seminars where people were studying/preparing themselves to become Waldorf teachers. There were also the visits to South Africa and the enlightening encounters there with many people who were at least as deeply absorbed in the 'kingdom' of Prester John and its implications for the Portuguese discoveries as I was. And even prior to all that was the lecture given in England by Norman Macbeth on 'The Deed of Portugal' which I had heard in the early 60s; lawyer as he was, he made out a magnificent case for the pre-eminence of Portugal at the beginning of the consciousness soul age. On the other hand, the call from Mexico came from the other half of the world that had been divided into two, so to speak, by Spain and Portugal, a half I confess I had not been particularly attracted to explore, either through reading or visiting, because of what Steiner's anthroposophical research had revealed.

Clearly, however, this was a turning point in my connection with the Waldorf scene in the Spanish-speaking world, a turning point poignantly confirmed by my arriving during the talks I gave on a possible history curriculum at the so-called Mexican mysteries—the shadow event of the Mystery of Golgotha,★ described by Steiner as being central in them—*exactly* on Good Friday. This coincidence was not planned. I have to admit that, through pressure of work, I had not closely followed the course of the Christian year after Epiphany in connection with the engagements in my diary.

On the human side, the heart-on-sleeve happiness and friendliness of all whom I met amongst the Cuernavaca school community enabled me to feel an instantly deep connection with the diaspora of Spanish culture. (Further links in the chain over the years took me to Peru, twice to Colombia, Spain itself and, as a climax of sorts, to establish and direct the first teacher training courses in the Canary Islands.) A host of incidents in Mexico that gave me the feeling of being 'at home' reside in the memory. For example, there was an occasion when, being driven through the glorious Mexican countryside, I commented that I must make more of an effort to get to know the geography of the land; my host (with the latest talk still fresh in mind) quipped: 'How about the *spiritual* geography?' On another occasion, parents of the school treated me to a 'free' weekend in Mexico City and I experienced a full-blown Mexican hotel breakfast; I was regaled with tortillas of various descriptions, swimming in scrambled eggs, and one of their tongue-

---

★ Steiner's frequently used expression for the earthly and cosmic significance of the events surrounding the first Easter.

scorching sauces. Then there was the occasion when I first relished what a siesta could do for one's constitution: after lunch my hosts pointed to the garden with its cascades of bougainvillaea and urged, 'You take the hammock.' Many times I had dinner under a moonlit sky with a crowd (so it seemed) of teachers, spouses, friends, children and other hangers-on gesticulating, dancing, joking, radiating life. Once, on my second visit, I was turfed along with other passengers, late at night, out of the airport onto the street; though facing what looked like a sea of faces and not knowing who would be meeting me, deep down (while I yet clung to my passport and wallet) I felt that all would be well. On another occasion, when I was being driven to school by a parent with a 9-year-old boy, the boy discovered his mother couldn't speak English, whereat he puzzled: 'Whatever did you do at school?' I remember on a visit being greeted by one of my host's sons, who imitated his father's bear-hug and fondly patted my shoulder. And there was the time when, too shy to refuse, I accepted an invitation to visit (yet another) archaeological ruin, which turned out to be good-ness knows how many metres climb and—kill or cure—I threw off impending flu. Lastly, there were all those occasions when the Mexicans' joyful boast that 'we spend half the time saying *Hola* and the other half saying *Hastar mañana*' came metaphorically true.

★ ★ ★

But amidst all the frivolity and excitement was the serious pursuit of the teachers to find the way of adapting Waldorf to a country far removed from the introverted attitudes to life north of the Alps. It was this that gave rise to the comment recalled at the head of the chapter.

On my second visit, I was asked to give a course on the

development of human consciousness as revealed in the history of the visual arts. The idea behind it was to complement what had been 'learnt' the year before with an exercise (looking at pictures of reliefs from the ancient Mexican temples and the like) that would induce an understanding of how human consciousness evolved. Thus the growing awareness resulting from the exercise would be applied to the local factors, looking for parallels as much as identifying distinctions.

I was more than happy to acquiesce, so I went along with my irreplaceable collection of slides in my hand luggage. But it was only when we came to 'set up shop' that the organizers realized the screen for the projector had been overlooked. Seeing that the table, spread with mouth-watering refreshments (juices, fruits, nibbles and cookies), had a white tablecloth, I suggested using it in place of a screen, as the distemper on the bare wall was off-white and would not have produced the best colour results. It was as we were fixing this up—in itself an extremely Heath Robinson affair—that a senior colleague commented with evident satisfaction, verging on the mischievous: 'He's getting quite Mexican!' The remark was meant as the pinnacle of compliments. I suppose that if you can't adapt a tablecloth to a projector screen, there's little chance that you will be able to shift the centre of gravity of your thinking from the stream of world history that becomes Euro-centric to a parallel stream, such as that which throve for millennia across the vast continents west of the Atlantic.

30. Achieving Waldorf

Confidence in the Unknown—Growth of the Waldorf
Movement in the UK and Ireland—Gaining Experience—
The Perception of Peers—Mentoring—Interviewing—
Research into TV's Devastating Side-effects

'How will we know?'
The property ladder and the career ladder both take some
climbing but they are essentially very different in character.
The latter is one of those tantalizing chicken-and-egg situations, in which you have acquired your qualifications and
then wait to see who will take you on *before* you have
arrived at that first rung of *experience*—a situation perhaps at
its most nail-biting in the acting profession. The former is
clear: you first need the 'goose' and will use the 'golden
egg' it has laid (*eggs*: increasingly plural in today's market)
to put down your payment for a mortgage. But *gaining
teaching experience*?

Another comparison: teaching and swimming. They are
similar in that you can read volumes about both, but until
you have dived into classroom or water you do not know
whether you will 'sink or swim'. And the dissimilarity? If you
sink in the swimming pool, the water (as far as we know!)
unconcernedly goes on being the water that it has always
been—upholding the buoyancy of solid matter, taking on the
shape that the solid matter with which it is in contact dictates,
moving (if circumstances permit) in a way that discloses its
inherent connection with life and so on. The sinking of the
unsuccessful swimmer—beyond the personal tragedy—is
seemingly neither here nor there. But the unsuccessful

teacher? With repercussions reaching far, perhaps, into children's lives?

A friend who had been class teaching in Scotland moved to a country where Waldorf education was very much in its infancy. Many would-be teachers flocked to its christening. The simile can be dangerously extended: as with baptism by complete submersion, they dived into teaching with inadequate training and would consult my friend often on a daily basis, many by long distance telephone calls. She sometimes seemed like a spar that the sinking teacher clutched at in order to get to that first rung on the career ladder. Little wonder that, out of responsibility towards all concerned, schools advertise for teachers with (at least, bottom rung) experience so that classes don't suffer from too many of the teacher's brave but belly-flopping attempts to dive into the sometimes treacherous currents of the schoolroom. This is not at all to ignore the suffering of the pedagogically unbuoyant and floundering teacher.

★ ★ ★

We're a strange mixture. We protest against the suffering of animals—that is the suffering they undergo at the hand of humans. We shout from the rooftops when scientists reveal the devastating effects of TV ('the medium not the message'); recent research claims it is linked to myopia, ADD (attention deficient disorder), diabetes, cancer, autism, Alzheimer's, numbed brains, obesity, couch potatoes, puberty acceleration, the suppression of melatonin, irregular sleep and so on. One of the leading researchers, Dr Aric Sigman, an associate fellow of the British Psychological Society and author of *Remotely Controlled: How Television is Damaging our Lives*, who had analysed 35 high-profile scientific studies, insisted that 'arguments over how educational programmes are were a distraction' in allowing children to be subjected to TV. The news of this research broke within a week of the Unicef tsunami! But instead of the heaps of TV sets extracted from children's bedrooms, which one might have expected to see appearing overnight in waste skips or on rubbish dumps, one cynically suspects that the classroom will continue to be where (in childhood) the problem is dumped. After all, 19 February 2007 (when the research was placed into the public domain) was by no means the first time that the problems connected with TV have been vividly flagged over recent years.

At the same time, we more or less take lying down the conveyer-belt dictating of the education system by 'officials' whose understanding of the soul-spirit nature of the child, judged by their deeds, would suggest little knowledge of that nature, and therefore equally little understanding of how that nature can suffer at the hands of ill-informed legislators and educationists. Yet we subject those getting on the first rung of the career ladder to the chicken-and-egg impossibility of 'do you have experience?' The probationary period that is attached to Qualified Teacher Status (and likewise to the Waldorf equivalent) is a pragmatic way of meeting the problem. The *interview* procedure in any Waldorf school that follows Steiner's advice in this respect is an attempt to get at least one step beyond the necessarily restricted pragmatic approach. It ensures that the whole teaching body, what is sometimes referred to as 'the College' (*Collegium*), not only decides on the appointment but sets up collegial support arrangements (such as mentoring) *within the school*, for the sake of the children just as much as for the teacher, to increase the swimming for newcomer while decreasing, or preferably pre-empting, any possible sinking.

Chicken-and-egg situations frequently occur when Waldorf finds itself in a new environment. Every family's first child to enter a Waldorf school poses the question of parental confidence. Even if the Maintained Sector *in the view of the parents* is riddled with problems—basic problems, not merely those hyped up by the media—there is still the lurking 'devil-you-know' kind of doubt to be confronted and dismissed before taking the plunge into the unknown. Does it conceal a devil you don't know? Or an angel?

In some countries Waldorf is a completely undiscovered planet for the majority of the population, distantly orbiting in the education system. A group is founded to look into the feasibility of introducing it. Perhaps an encouraging number of people rally round the banner—as was the case remarkably with the teacher training course which took place in La Gomera (Canary Islands) in 2004–6.★ However, with the nearest complete Waldorf school being several hours plane flight away, it is not likely that the course will be followed with schools springing up like mushrooms overnight. (The early years initiatives that have resulted, nevertheless, hold promise for the future.)

Or there is the well-known situation of a new school being opened in a country where Waldorf has been known for decades. Until 1970, the education was practised in England in literally a mere handful of schools, the first having been founded in London in January 1925 with Steiner's enthusiastic support and encouragement. But during those 45 years, despite Upper Schools having been established in them all, the growth factor was far from mushrooming. Then four

---

★ The enrolment was about 0.015% of the population of the island. The Waldorf teacher training course in London, by comparison, attracts only 0.00001% of the population, though this is an annual intake. The ratio of La Gomera to London works out as approximately 1000:1!

new schools opened, priming the pump for the next spurt of growth. Yet only one of them to date (2007) has achieved a full Upper School. Perhaps the rhythm in the UK and Ireland is a 45-year rhythm and we still have another ten years to wait before we see any hatching out of the chicken and egg dilemmas.

★   ★   ★

Once, in the late 90s, when I was teaching main-lesson to a Class 12, I came to the conclusion that British hesitance in spiritual matters (if that's what underlies the phenomenon) must be a national—multinational?—trait and not merely the understandable cautiousness of parents choosing schooling that is going to set their children up for life. ('Waldorf? Children *enjoying* school?' Or the all too typical reaction: 'Beware of anything new-fangled!') This mental inertia does not appear to exist in Germany where education broadly speaking has been a serious part of people's outlook on life, something frequently extending right into one's twenties, and where the formidable philosophy behind Waldorf has been decoy enough for the movement to thrive in an unprecedented way. In addition, many satellites have arisen—the voluminous secondary literature, educational magazines for parents that focus on Waldorf, firms manufacturing wholesome food and clothing, toys and children's furniture, etc., an ambience which is a far cry from the Iwate Government's (north Japan) teachers' manual, headlined in a *TES* (Times Educational Supplement) report as 'Monster Parents', which severely warns teachers against getting sucked into disputes that are the results of 'American-style individualism' spreading through the country.

Once of the outcomes of Waldorf that Steiner envisaged was that its full spectrum might be recognized as an equivalent to University Entrance. This was pointedly expressed on one occasion when he urged: '*Achieve* Waldorf!' He labelled the thirteenth class, where pupils could be prepared for entrance to university, an 'exam preparation' class. This implies that the twelve-year Waldorf curriculum could be safeguarded from exam-style encroachment and therefore developed into a foundation for higher education that could be recognized, alongside others. But it is not an either/or situation. His 'achieve Waldorf' was in fact a response to improving the State exam results.

The Waldorf school in Mount Barker, Australia was among the first to achieve this Higher Education recognition status, I discovered during my visit there in 1991. Hardly a precedent that British universities would be impelled by, but I thought it worth a try and, to that end, began negotiations with the University of Roehampton. To cut a long story short, the protocol was in its final stages of preparation at the time I was teaching the Class 12 main-lesson mentioned above. I sought the opinion of members of the class, who were, as it happened, in the throes of A levels, but who I thought would be objective enough—maybe even their objectivity fortuitously spurred by the A-level preparative experience—to reflect accurately the mood of the actual 'lambs to the slaughter'. It wasn't a discussion, of course, that I could justify holding during school time, since it was an initiative promoted by myself personally in conjunction with the university, so I invited those who were interested to meet me in a corner of the canteen in the second half of the lunch break. Their response was positive but guarded—which reassured me of the objectivity kicking in.

Leaving the positive on one side, it is the guarded aspect that is pertinent here—surely, I reflected, stemming from the inherent, chicken-and-eggy pragmatism of the English psyche. 'How will we know,' they questioned, envisaging the situation of *not* having to go through the exam grind, 'that we are on a par with those who will be our peers, once we are at university?' They needed more than a 'time will soon tell' answer, which would be unlikely to convince if given in a glib way. But what interested me was the slight flicker of hope that pragmatism can be defeated. This was evident in the leaning towards adventure that you expect of youth expressed in the formulation they used: not the somewhat abstract, disengaged and tinged with incredulity 'How would we know?' but 'How *will* we know?'

31. The Sense-perceptible World and its Counterpart

Mathematics—Rubicon—Apartheid—Maths Phobia—
Measurable—Immeasurable

'Would you like a cup of tea?'
I was tutoring a boy who was prevented from attending school due to an accident. Tutoring sounds too princely. I merely deputized for his appointed tutor who was unable to cancel a prior engagement. But the circumstances were unusual. The first I heard of it was a phone call close to midnight—not something you normally respond to unless you are expecting some such call, but on impulse I lifted the receiver rather than let the caller get trapped in the dreaded *mail voice box facility*. (What linguistic contortions we are prepared to go through to kid ourselves that our ever-dwindling person-to-person lifestyle is not undermining our humanity, individually, culturally and in society as a whole!) Be that as it may, on this occasion the phone call facilitated two male voices—the tutor's and that of a small boy at the Rubicon stage—coming into dialogue in an educational context. (More about the 'box' where it all happened later.)

The tutoring hours for which I was to be responsible were scheduled for the following afternoon. This gave me time to prepare, after the midnight briefing I had had—so-called 'cover lessons' are notorious for their brief briefings—and get myself to London. Thinking it over, the situation had a touch of the Rubicon challenge about it for me—facing a brand new situation—a call at midnight, *afternoon* teaching hours, and a pupil who would benefit from keeping regular subjects like English and maths ticking over until he had recovered sufficiently to rejoin his class. Afternoon (the time for *will* activities, if you take seriously Steiner's view of child development and its application to the school timetable), the frequently grinding approach to numeracy and the unadorned nuts and bolts of literacy do not immediately strike one as a match for one another predestined in heaven. So here was a recipe for the compounding of the situation regarding 'core' subjects, which is well known to all of us in the profession, if we're honest. It's all too easy to teach (for example, spelling or long division) so that pupils feel constantly confronted with the threat of correct or incorrect, tick or cross, right or wrong, black or white.

I have written extensively about literacy elsewhere,★ so here will confine myself to the potentially traumatic aspect of numeracy.

★ ★ ★

I recall from my own schooldays a case in point. A friend in my class would inwardly cringe as the maths master appeared at the classroom doorway. Here was another of those agonizing experiences pending: frantic and confused labour usually resulting in a disgustingly blotted page, followed by a bombardment of red ink crosses, one targeted at each answer. In order to avoid the dreaded confrontation, he once made the fatal mistake of copying his neighbour's imposing display of ticked answers—I won't discuss the fatal mistake that must

---

★ See the author's 'The Spirit or the Letter—On Whose Side is the Teacher of Literacy Fighting?' in *The Future is Now: Anthroposophy at the New Millennium* pp. 157–73, Temple Lodge, London 1999; and *Adventures in Steiner Education: an Introduction to the Waldorf Approach*, Sophia Books, Forest Row 2005.

have gnawed at the core of the teacher's pedagogy. There is, of course, the slim chance that it was just 'the system' at fault, but if I tell you we nicknamed the teacher 'Tank' you might get a hint of the true flavour. So armed with his cribbed answers and relishing the thought of ticks to come, my friend joined the queue that led to the high altar—the teacher's 'desk' on raised dais where, draped voluminously in his chalk-smudged, ominously black academic gown, he held court and dispensed red-ticked elation where it was due or, where it was not, red-crossed misery, without much in between it seemed. Alas, my friend's ruse didn't stand a chance of penetrating 'Tank's' armoured plating. When it came to his turn to have his book marked, his pounding heart and anxious soul were greeted with neither ticks nor crosses. With poised pen in one hand and, giving time for considered response while adjusting his spectacles with the other hand, as he scrutinized the proffered page, the maths tyrant (as he must have seemed to my friend) ploughed a heavy red diagonal furrow across the entire page of sums, from bottom left to top right, with barely a crease on the facial skin to indicate any remote sense of fellow feeling. As he did so, he drawled so that the whole class couldn't avoid 'savouring' the ignominy: 'Answers right, working wrong, *eyesight good*.'

Eureka! How to bring *feeling* into maths, so that, even if the correct figures don't fall into the consciousness as instantly as acorns pelting down from an autumn oak, the feeling will be engendered of *wanting* to achieve, to strive on, to climb the unyieldingly towering north face and gain the view from the summit. (I am doing my best to present an accurate estimation of how psychologically exposed it can feel at that mathematically feared red-cross 'base camp'.)

Competence in the subject can also be used to sort out what are deemed to be the sheep from the goats, though I shall leave the reader to judge which of the species in an 'animal farm' they would prefer to be ruled by. A colleague who had taught mathematics in South Africa at the time of the most stringent apartheid regime recounted the following. She was enjoying her teaching—was content to be 'in education' and in all modesty felt she was doing a reasonable job. Then one day it dawned on her. Putting two and two together (an irresistible idiom in the circumstances!) she worked out that a big factor in the head-hunting by which those who were the sternest adherents and most powerfully relentless executors of apartheid arrived at the 'top of the pile' was their proven ability in maths. Needless to say, feeling played no part in the head-hunting, or at least not equal feelings of empathy with *all* inhabitants of the country. She needed no Desmond Tutu to prick her conscience, and resigned forthwith. There's the rub: the hard, black-and-white, no-grey-area of it all. The subject can be as white as pure snow yet as cold and forbidding as Hans Christian Andersen's 'The Snow Queen', especially if it is rigorously and oppressively restricted to 'from the neck up'.

This may seem an overly discursive preamble to the point I am making about the pedagogical treacherousness of maths teaching, but it is easy for the teacher—even the one who genuinely enjoys his subject and his job—to forget that *those same waters*, which he is relishing during the balmy time he is spending surfing at a Florida beach, are frozen ice-caps not many thousands of miles away. The pedagogy of maths teaching needs 'global warming' if it is going to reach the hearts of slow- as well as quick-minded pupils—and *both* types need the warmth: the slower pupils so that they are given the necessary time it takes to get to enjoy the waves breaking on the shores of numeracy, and the quicker ones so that any inherent tendency in their makeup to global-*freezing*

is countered. Steiner himself, seer that he was, was as self–
disciplined as they come in the purely logical mental sphere
to which, among others, mathematics arguably belongs (viz.
his higher education training predominantly in the sciences),
in his consciousness thus being on a different plane to the
mystic that he is sometimes mistaken for.

So how can *number* touch the feelings of a young reluctant
'mathematician'? An encouraging way, widely used in
Waldorf circles, is through discovering the *numerically rhythmic patterns* that exist. A glimpse into this secret garden is
already experienced when children start to count. This is
usually something that comes from the child's inner participation in everyday life: the joy of birthdays as landmarks in
the rising age of the child (you don't need to be a quick
thinker in order to form the concept of advancing from four
to five!); the 'speedier' four candles on the Advent wreath
being lit week by week as the light increases towards
Christmas or, similarly, day by day for the eight candles of
Hanukkah, and suchlike celebrations; the even quicker
numerical 'digesting' of two or three pieces of toast for
breakfast—and there is the comparatively hidden sevenfold
cycle in the days of the week and such rhythms connected
with the starry heavens. These and other similar experiences
lay the foundations for the child's personal relationship with
the world of number.

Building on these life-experience foundations, therefore,
the teacher will be on solid ground if she taps into the
rhythmical life of number: initially the sheer fascination of
counting aloud (up *and* down), the discovery of the common
every-other-one rhythm (2, 4, 6, 8...), the friendly famil-
iarity feeling of how a similar pattern surfaces in tens or
elevens (20, 30, 40, 50 ... or 22, 33, 44, 55...). Seeing
numbers written down in the first class, the discovery of the

four processes and such basics in numeracy are well worth spending time on and approaching *imaginatively and tangibly*. This can be done through movement and through the handling of pleasing objects taken from nature (e.g. medium-sized sea-shells, shiny grained horse-chestnuts, or kidney beans) so that all the children—again just as much the quicker as the slower ones—can discover their own deep relationship with numbers, feel it in their bones, so to speak. Steiner even saw the human's propensity for living in that world as being part of each person's birthright. (Not so with literacy, interestingly enough.) The teacher's task is to help each child discover the key that unlocks that propensity—a key that is right under the nose of the so-called gifted child; but at the other extreme, the search can be long and arduous.

★ ★ ★

In the third class (age 8/9) a further step in grounding numeracy can be taken when the smaller/bigger, lighter/heavier, faster/slower, wider/narrower, fuller/emptier, more/less aspects of life start to be quantified. The metric and imperial roads of measurement then will lead from inches and centimetres, pints and litres, ounces and grams, crochets and quarter notes to other measuring units in later years, such as those used to quantify air pressure, bank rates, acreage, currency, molecular structure, electric current, earthquake tremors, altitude, longitude, hard disk capacity, map references and a thousand others. For, as humans conquer the world, ever new footsteps of mensuration, statistical research, empirical evidence, etc. become dinted into the expanding continents of knowledge. It's not difficult to see how those footsteps can therefore lead to a world view that is obsessed with and blinkered by sense-perception—weigh it, measure it, time it, analyse it . . .

The inner life, fortunately, proceeds differently. Being non-measurable, we can afford to think of it as potentially immeasurable. Sadly, however, especially for the Gradgrind mode of intelligence that admits only facts, its out-of-sight-out-of-mindness, its very spirituality, often consigns it to the irrelevant. Yet the *awareness* of it that could be accessible to the man in the street, for Steiner, was sparked off at a very fundamental level when he, already as a schoolboy, realized that all constructed or otherwise manufactured triangles (and today he would surely have included electronically produced samples) can only approximate to the absolute perfection of the *purely imagined* one. Strangely and remarkably enough, this realization gave him hope that all people, having such an experience in common and, given an unprejudiced and open-minded attitude to life, can therefore recognize and acknowledge that there *is* such a sphere of existence as the metaphysical. Never mind, in the first place, about the somewhat awkward reality of its being *purer* than the sphere of quantitative (physical) existence, a consideration of which would take us towards the conquering of the inner 'man', a vital yet lagging behind complementary activity to the conquering of the forces in the material world. In view of this, dispelling (or better, pre-empting) maths phobia is a vital task for the teacher, for the sake of both the inner and outer 'man'.

Seen from this point of view, the maths teacher's task can make a meaningful contribution to life as a whole, the early stages of which are vital. They will very largely determine whether the mountain spring of numeracy will flow generously to bring fertility to each one's biographical landscape—borrower or lender, teacher or student, butcher, baker or candlestick maker, king or commoner—or (please not) disappear into some wadi of disinterest. Hence, to return to my visit to London: my young tutee and I spent an engaging couple of literacy/numeracy hours or so, first savouring the beauty of language and then clapping, counting, reciting numbers rhythmically, 'discovering' number patterns and diving thereby into various 'operations', etc. At the end (a happily spontaneous end, entirely his own initiative) he gentlemanly enquired—and in a cultured voice seldom found in Rubicon-aged boys—'Would you like a cup of tea?' While we drank juice and tea, chatted and nibbled cookies, his younger brother arrived back hungry from school, and it was soon time for me to depart. As I descended the sweeping staircase I noticed a portrait hanging on the wall, which had escaped my attention on the way in. I must have had my back to it as I went up to the improvised schoolroom. It was a large and striking portrait—certainly, as is the whole incident, life-size in my memory—of Diana, Princess of Wales, his mother.

Epilogue: Education is Lifesaving

Through the kind concession of the publisher, I enjoyed an arrangement by which, up until the end of the copy-editing stage of the present work, I would be able to add inserts of relevant research to the submitted manuscript. The reason for this was that, while the book aimed to be of medium-term value—and considering that 'modern issues' have a habit of resurfacing over years or even decades—the very latest light could be shed, the latest voice could be heard, the latest overshadowing cloud could be detected, the latest examples could be cited, and so forth.

At the eleventh hour (eleven days to be precise) before this arrangement had to be terminated, the *Times Educational Supplement* of 6 July 2007 published a short article extolling the career of Peter Richards OBE who had been short listed, after 40 years 'at the chalk face', for the Ted Wragg award for a lifetime achievement in education. Among the issues highlighted was his view on the problems of religious fundamentalism (in all its guises). What particularly caught my eye, however—it would be truer to say my 'ear'—was his concluding 'Education is our lifesaver'. The first reason I had for using his expression at the heading of this final 'chapter' (slightly changed) was my perception of his voice being a fairly lone one—I am tempted to add 'crying in the wilderness'—since it was clear he meant *education* as distinct from the testing of it, the funding of it, the league tables appertaining to it, the knife-culture policing of it, the political 'Education, Education, Education' vote-attracting usefulness of it, the intellectual blinkers with which it is usually viewed, the pressured surveillance of it, the increasing vulture-like atmosphere in the shape of litigation surrounding it and so on. The second reason was my astonishment that his perception of education was expressed in terms of *lifesaving*. If only it had been a feature article with a multitude of illustrative details of what he had in mind!

The mental block that appears to exist when it comes to education as such sometimes beggars belief. At the end of June 2007, reports of the Herefordshire County Council's rejection of plans for a Steiner 'academy' in the county gave the reason simply as there being 'no need for additional school places'. Of course, there will be those who take the harsh view: Serve it right: the academy shouldn't have indicated that it might concede to keystage testing, but stuck to its guns as a kosher Steiner establishment. At the same time, one can't help wondering if the councillors' thinking rose any further than 'bums-on-seats' type of pragmatism. If it did, it doesn't appear to be reflected in their negative decision.

It is, of course, for others to judge for themselves which approaches to education they consider are of human worth (in Richards's evolutionary, lifesaving sense), but I have frequently been heartened by the view of Owen Barfield, the intellectual sparring partner of C.S. Lewis, with whom, beside Tolkien and others, he sat in The Bird and Baby (as the pub The Eagle and Child was endearingly referred to) and discussed, disputed and contended, while puffing at his pipe as a member of the renowned Oxford University 'Inklings' circle. Writing of Waldorf education in the latter part of his long, distinguished and phenomenally productive life he concluded: 'I have always felt a deep concern, simply as a human being, with the possible success or failure of Waldorf education. It appears to me to be deeply bound up with the possible success or failure of Western civilization, if not of humanity itself as an institution.'*

Tolkien's gift to childhood, particularly in *Lord of the Rings* was, I would say, of an epic nature, while C.S. Lewis's popular story books have, linguistically and in other ways, something of a lyrical tendency. Completing the trio, there could be little that is more dramatic than Barfield's perception of Waldorf education's potential contribution to childhood and the further evolution of humanity, a drama largely begun with the raising of the curtain of the twentieth century and still being fiercely enacted over the issues of our time. The issues pose constantly front of stage—clear for all to see— bludgeoning our peace of mind, undermining our creativity, threatening our health and safety, fanning our fears, moth-eating our budgets, taking the wind out of the sails of our imaginative thinking, topsy-turvying our lives, 'damaging' our children. It is high time, surely, that the naked *educational* implications stepped out from the wings.

Brien Masters
Midsummer 2007

---

* See *Owen Barfield: A Waldorf Tribute*, a Steiner Education Monograph, ISBN 0 9530101 1 2.

Appendix: Press Letter on Toxic Childhood

The text of the letter appearing in the *Daily Telegraph* on 12 September 2006 is given in full on a web page maintained by one of the letter's two organizers, Dr Richard House of Roehampton University's Research Centre for Therapeutic Education. He can be contacted on *r.house@roehampton.ac.uk*. Ideas and feedback are welcomed.

As professionals and academics from a range of backgrounds, we are deeply concerned at the escalating incidence of childhood depression and children's behavioural and developmental conditions. We believe this is largely due to a lack of understanding, on the part of both politicians and the general public, of the realities and subtleties of child development.

Since children's brains are still developing, they cannot adjust—as full-grown adults can—to the effects of ever more rapid technological and cultural change. They still need what developing human beings have always needed, including real food (as opposed to processed 'junk'), real play (as opposed to sedentary, screen-based entertainment), first-hand experience of the world they live in and regular interaction with the real-life significant adults in their lives.

They also need time. In a fast-moving hyper-competitive culture, today's children are expected to cope with an ever-earlier start to formal schoolwork and an overly academic test-driven primary curriculum. They are pushed by market forces to act and dress like mini-adults and exposed via the electronic media to material which would have been considered unsuitable for children even in the very recent past.

Our society rightly takes great pains to protect children from physical harm, but seems to have lost sight of their emotional and social needs. However, it's now clear that the mental health of an unacceptable number of children is being unnecessarily compromised, and that this is almost certainly a key factor in the rise of substance abuse, violence and self-harm amongst our young people.

This is a complex socio-cultural problem to which there is no simple solution, but a sensible 'first step' would be to encourage parents and policy-makers to start talking about ways of improving children's well-being. We therefore propose as a matter of urgency that

- public debate be initiated on child-rearing in the 21st century
- this issue should be central to public policy-making in coming decades.

[Any readers wishing to contribute to this debate can contact us by logging on to: http://ipnosis.postle.net/childhood.htm]

Yours sincerely

[Over a hundred signatories are listed in alphabetical order.]

Index

ALSO IN THE 'BRINGING SPIRIT TO LIFE' SERIES:

Adventures in Steiner Education, An Introduction to the Waldorf Approach
Brien Masters

A Child is Born, A Natural Guide to Pregnancy, Birth and Early Childhood
Wilhelm zur Linden

From Stress to Serenity, Gaining Strength in the Trials of Life
Angus Jenkinson

Homemaking as a Social Art, Creating a Home for Body, Soul and Spirit
Veronika van Duin

The Journey Continues . . ., Finding a New Relationship to Death
Gilbert Childs with Sylvia Childs

Meditation, Transforming our lives for the encounter with Christ
Jörgen Smit

Raising the Soul, Practical Exercises for Personal Development
Warren Lee Cohen

Well I Wonder . . ., Childhood in the Modern World, A Handbook for Parents, Carers and Teachers
Sally Schweizer

Your Reincarnating Child, Welcoming a Soul to the World
Gilbert Childs and Sylvia Childs